Business Result

W0036206

Skills for Business Studies

Advanced

Jon Naunton

OXFORD

UNIVERSITY PRESS

Contents

Managing globally

Study focus

1 Some people believe that a period spent working abroad can advance their careers. How true do you think this is?

2 What qualities do you think human resources managers look for when they are choosing people for overseas postings?

3 What challenges do employees and their families commonly face when they are posted overseas? How can they be prepared for what lies ahead?

Reading strategies

A | Reading quickly for general understanding

1 **Which sentence best summarizes the text?**

The text …
a provides an overview of how companies adapt when they set up a branch abroad.
b describes the consequences of cultural misunderstandings.
c discusses the qualities needed to settle into a new culture.

2 **Which person named in the text … ?**

a claims people have 'multiple selves'

b immersed himself in his business partners' artistic culture

c has a theory about Korea's success

d gained insights into the host culture through sport

e avoided work colleagues at the weekend

B | Identifying the writer's point of view

Answer the questions.

1 In recent times, why has it become more difficult for senior executives to avoid an overseas' posting?

2 What does the author think of the steps that companies often take to help managers adapt to a new culture?

3 Why does the writer think that 'transcultural' is a better way than 'global' to describe international managers?

4 What does he mean when he says that transcultural mangers have both 'roots and wings'?

5 Why does he consider that learning a few words in a foreign language, or 'mastering the perfect bow' are superficial activities?

6 Why does the writer believe that the extra effort people make is worthwhile?

7 According to the writer, what transformation occurs within the most successful international managers?

C | Critical evaluation

Discuss these questions.

• How convincing do you find the distinction that the author draws between the *global manager* and a *transcultural manager*?

• How seriously should we take Zachary's theory about Korea's recent success, and Japan's relative decline? What other possible explanations can you think of?

• The author of the article depends on subjects 'self-reporting'; i.e. describing their own experiences.
  – How valid and reliable is this type of evidence?
  – How far should we trust it?

• On a scale of 1–10 how interesting/convincing do you find the ideas contained in the article? (0 = not at all; 10 = totally)

The transcultural manager

A More than ever before, senior executives and managers are required to spend time overseas as part of their work, ranging from short business trips to lengthy postings. The experience can be very difficult,
5 particularly in countries with different languages and customs. Yet the relentless beat of globalisation means that postings abroad are inevitable for many senior managers in large firms.

B A recent study of 270 CEOs of the companies that
10 comprise Standard and Poors/Toronto Stock Exchange index revealed that 40% had worked outside their home country, up from 29% only a decade ago. The numbers are even higher in Europe. Many companies try to help executives by offering language courses, relocation
15 training and brief courses on cultural differences. But while these can be useful activities, research suggests that they cannot create the mindset required to survive and thrive in a foreign culture. To achieve this, companies must go much deeper.

C The phrase 'global manager' has been coined to describe somebody who operates successfully across different cultures, but this suggests a person that does not and cannot really exist. Everyone is rooted in a particular culture, and where we grow up has a
25 profound impact on how we view the world. There is no 'global' management style that can be applied in any country and so no global managers. This is why the term 'transcultural executive' is a more appropriate term than global manager. A transcultural executive is
30 one who is at home in two or more cultures, someone who can cut across cultures.

D In a sense, transcultural managers are living paradoxes. They manage to have roots and wings. They have roots in their own home culture, ones in which they often take
35 considerable pride, yet they have travelled and lived in other parts of the world. Their wings have taken them elsewhere and allowed them to develop a real comfort in one or more different cultures, allowing them to have multiple selves. This is not an entirely new idea.
40 In his 1890 classic, *Principles of Psychology*, William James used the metaphor of multiple selves to describe human life. Rather than a single unified self-concept, he suggested that people have multiple selves that they demonstrate in various situations.

E After interviewing hundreds of managers who had spent considerable time working outside their home culture, one discovery struck me with considerable force. Being a transcultural executive goes significantly beyond surface activities such as learning a smattering
50 of a foreign language or mastering the perfect bow. Being transcultural means developing a mindset that reflects a deep respect for other cultures and a willingness to study them and learn what makes them

tick. It contains a genuine authentic interest in and
55 appreciation of the other culture, and a willingness to adopt that culture as an alternative self. It is a less important self; a winged self rather than a rooted self.

F But how do you become this unusual creature? Leaving behind the safety and comfort of your rooted self to
60 become a winged self involves hard work and sacrifice. Norbert Luebben, a German *Lufthansa* manager who has lived in London for four years has a simple rule: 'No *Lufthansa* people at the weekend.' He and his partner spend their weekends socialising with British people.
65 In the early days this made Luebben uncomfortable; he says he felt like a 'homesick ten-year-old' and longed for the comfort of familiar things. However, four years later he has become an anglophile and feels very much at home in a British culture. He can put on his British
70 self with ease. In fact, he does it unconsciously and can shift from his German self to his British self simply by hanging up the phone and talking to his English colleagues. Michi Sugawar, a marketing executive at *Fujitsu*, lived in Australia for four years. He found that a
75 good way to understand his Australian colleagues was to watch Australian sports: Australian Rules football, cricket and rugby. Not only did it give him something to talk about with his work colleagues, it also gave him insight into the Australian view of life.

G Being truly transcultural means going beyond just making friends. It means digging deeper into a culture and delving into its history, music and art. When you

engage in a culture at this more profound level, you will have more insight into its values. It is important that
85 you are seen to be going beyond the surface. Michael MacAdoo, vice-president of strategy at *Bombardier Aerospace*, had to go to China. Rather than taking on the difficult task of learning Mandarin, he spent considerable time reading up on Chinese history and
90 literature. His Chinese colleagues appreciated his respect for their history, but were even more impressed by his interest in Chinese art and literature.

H What can happen is that a person, in effect, becomes multi-cultural within themselves. In his book *The*
95 *Diversity Advantage: Multicultural identity in the new world economy* (2003), G.Pascal Zachary argues that the very best international managers hold different identities simultaneously. They make an effort to develop a deep understanding of a place
100 and incorporate some of their host culture into their own personality, but they also retain their own backgrounds and identities.

I The benefits can extend beyond the individual to companies and even entire countries. Korean
105 electronics firm *Samsung* has enjoyed higher profits in recent years than its Japanese rivals *Sony*, *Toshiba* and *Hitachi*. Its success can be partially traced to its 'transcultural philosophy' says Zachary. 'Korean firms

are very open. They have foreigners in senior positions
110 and actively seek to become more cosmopolitan. Japanese firms still tend to be dominated by Japanese people at senior levels even overseas. You could argue that Japan's stagnation in recent years has been due partly to this conservatism.' The thrust of Zachary's
115 argument is that becoming transcultural, whether at an individual or corporate level, is a process of hybridisation rather than homogenisation. 'You don't try to create uniformity,' he says. 'You learn to hold different identities at the same time and be comfortable
120 with that.'

Source: The transcultural manager, Karl Moore. 2006 *The World Business*

Glossary

anglophile (line 68): a lover of things connected to England and the English way of life

hybridisation (line 117): the process of combining elements from different sources to create something new

inevitable (line 07): not possible to avoid or prevent something from happening

stagnation (line 113): a period where there is little or no growth in business activity

thrive (line 18): to do a lot of business and grow

Business vocabulary

A | Crossing cultures

1 Check that you understand the following key terms 1–9 from the text. Match them to the correct definition a–i.

1 posting ___
2 mindset ___
3 homogenisation ___
4 bow ___
5 paradox ___
6 smattering ___
7 host culture ___
8 cosmopolitan ___
9 insight ___

a the form of greeting used in Japan and China
b an understanding of the true nature of something
c a job elsewhere, often abroad
d with people or ideas from all over the world
e a person's established way of thinking
f a contradiction that is nevertheless true
g knowledge of a few words in a foreign language
h the process of making everything the same
i the customs and traditions of the country that receives you

2 Complete the sentences using the words from 1.

1 It may seem like a _____, but the most difficult time for an executive who has lived abroad is when he comes back home.

2 She speaks a _____ of Mandarin and Cantonese that makes a good first impression.

3 The handshake has replaced the _____ in a lot of business situations.

4 We need to change our _____ and think more creatively.

5 A foreign _____ can be a good way of developing your staff.

6 The training course gave me a useful _____ into how Russians negotiate.

7 If you can't feel a certain sympathy with the _____ you'll never settle in.

8 We have a _____ team with people from all around the world.

9 Don't be fooled by what seems to be the _____ of international culture. Once you break through the surface you'll see just how differently people think.

B | Verbs with prepositions and adverbs

1 **Complete the definitions by matching 1–8 to a–h.**

1 If we *delve into* something, … ___
2 If we *long for* something, … ___
3 When something *cuts across* separate groups, … ___
4 If we *leave something behind* us, … ___
5 When we *go beyond* something, … ___
6 If we *engage in* something, … ___
7 When something *tends to* happen, … ___
8 If something *ranges from* something to something else, … ___

a we take part in it seriously.
b it has variations between two points or amounts.
c we abandon an old place or way of life.
d experience tells us it is likely.
e we want it very much.
f we exceed it, or are better in some way.
g it affects them all in a similar way.
h we try hard to find out more about it.

2 **What would you say in the following situations? Use expressions from 1 to rephrase these sentences.**

1 Our service deals with everything from cultural training and language lessons for new recruits, and helping their families settle in through to de-briefing them at the end of their contracts.

_____

_____

2 We were delighted with the training programme – it was more than we expected.

_____

_____

3 We need to carry out some in-depth research to discover why staff don't renew their contracts.

_____

_____

4 When Gabrielle went to work in New York she changed everything about her appearance.

_____

_____

5 I really can't wait to be sent abroad, I am fed up with working in London.

_____

_____

6 If you want extra time for your assignment, ask her after the lecture. She is usually more relaxed then.

_____

_____

7 The recession has affected all different segments of the economy.

_____

_____

8 It's time we took the problems posed by culture shock more seriously.

_____

_____

Writing skills

| Writing a summary

Summary writing skills are important. By being able to summarize a longer text and express another person's ideas in your own words shows you have a good understanding of theories and ideas.

1 **Discuss comments 1–6 with a partner. Which statements are true or false?**

A good summary …
1 should use the exact words of the original text.
   True ___   False ___
2 should be much shorter in length.
   True ___   False ___
3 can introduce ideas from other sources.
   True ___   False ___
4 should focus on key ideas and not detail.
   True ___   False ___
5 should include your own opinion.
   True ___   False ___
6 should make judgements about the content.
   True ___   False ___

2 Match headings a–f to sections 1–6 in the Useful expressions box.

a Listing and enumerating points
b Giving the writer's opinions
c Saying where something is from
d Introducing an alternative viewpoint
e Referring to the writer's sources
f Saying 'but'/making contrasts

Useful expressions

Writing a summary

1 ___

This extract/passage is (taken) from …
It appears/was published in …

2 ___

It cites research by …
The work of X receives special mention.
X is extensively quoted …
He quotes/mentions X …
He refers to X's work on …

3 ___

The writer takes issue with/objects to …
The author maintains, argues, suggests, implies …

4 ___

although
despite/despite the fact
however
while
by contrast

5 ___

Nevertheless
However, there seems to be little hard evidence to support this claim.

6 ___

Firstly/to begin with
Secondly
In addition
Furthermore
Finally

---

3 Study a student's notes on paragraph B of the reading text on page 5. Look back at paragraph B and underline the main idea they have used.

Standard and Poors/Toronto Stock Exchange found people work out of home country. Esp Europe. Help for execs = lang + cult courses. Research = not effective

4 Which phrases have been used from 2 to expand these notes to a summary?

The writer refers to Standard and Poors/Toronto Stock Exchange's study on the increasing number of people working in other countries, particularly in Europe. Although extensive training is often provided, the writer argues that, on its own, this is not effective.

5 Take notes on paragraphs C and D. Focus on main ideas only and use short forms and symbols to keep your notes brief.

6 Compare your notes with a partner and expand them into a summary.

Research task

1 People sometimes compare a new culture to an iceberg. Find out what this metaphor means.

2 What are the visible and invisible parts of the cultural iceberg?

3 Choose a well-known multinational enterprise (MNE) and find out how it prepares staff and their families for international postings.

4 How, if at all, does the MNE help with reverse 'culture shock'? (Reverse culture shock occurs when someone returns to their original culture after a period away.)

2 Uncertain careers

Study focus

1 For you, what is the difference between a job and a career?

2 How many jobs or occupations do you think you will have during your working life?

3 How have career expectations changed since your parents' and grandparents' day?

Reading strategies

A | Predicting content from topic sentences

A topic sentence is the sentence in any paragraph which gives an overview of the main point of that paragraph. Identifying and understanding the topic sentence is key to understanding the rest of the paragraph.

1 **These are the topic sentences from the text on page 10. Read them and predict what the rest of the paragraph might say.**

Paragraph A
Most people face obstacles and setbacks in their careers, and many employees, blue collar and white collar, change their jobs and even their occupations several times over their working lives.

Paragraph B
However, managerial careers in the 1980s and 1990s have been less stable and predictable in developed Western countries than they were in the period between 1950 and 1980.

Paragraph C
Career satisfaction is a result of an individual's identification with home and work roles; performing them successfully, and being able to meet new challenges.

Paragraph D
In the USA and the UK during the 1980s, it became more common for people to feel that stable careers no longer existed and that organizations were unable any longer to offer a job for life.

Paragraph E
The *old deal* was a relational contract whereby each party – employer and employee – learnt to trust one another over time.

Paragraph F
Increasing competitive pressures in general and change in national governments' policy faced by multinational and national organizations have both contributed to eroding the ability of employers to fulfil their side of the bargain under the terms of the *old deal*.

2 Read each paragraph in full and compare your answers from 1.

B | Reading for detailed understanding

Which statements are true (T) or false (F) according to the text?

1 Despite life changes people's views of themselves are remarkably stable.
T ___   F ___

2 Successful managers often show early signs of success.
T ___   F ___

3 Managerial careers have always suffered from uncertainty.
T ___   F ___

4 In recent decades, most organizations' hierarchical ladders have become much shorter.
T ___   F ___

5 People are less motivated to seek promotion than they used to be.
T ___   F ___

6 Career satisfaction relies on balancing competing demands.
T ___   F ___

7 People should seek outside help to deal with a personal career crisis.
T ___   F ___

8 The notion of what is meant by a 'career' changed some time in the 1970s.
T ___   F ___

9 The 'old deal' relied on mutual confidence between employers and employees.
T ___   F ___

10 The 'old deal' had more sympathy towards human weakness.
T ___   F ___

11 Staff with technical or scientific 'know-how' still benefit from greater job security.
T ___   F ___

12 Nowadays, employers and employees are much more calculating than they used to be.
T ___   F ___

The changing psychological contract

A ___ As people's experience of life changes over time, they adjust to some extent to their concept of self and personal identity. There are some conventionally successful individuals whose careers progress relatively
5 smoothly and develop in a linear and 'upwardly mobile' fashion. John Kotter's 1982 study of general managers in the US found common factors for success; it seems to be connected with achievements at an early age and major responsibility being attained before the
10 individual is in his or her mid-thirties.

B ___ Fundamental changes in government policy, especially concerning privatization and de-regulation, have combined with greater competitive pressures, causing many large corporate organizations to flatten
15 or 'de-layer' their managerial hierarchies, to 'downsize', and to subcontract what are considered peripheral services. One consequence of the reduction in levels of the organizational hierarchy for employees is that, in both the public and private sector, there is less
20 incentive to seek hierarchical promotion. There now exists in organizations, less opportunity for promotion, social advancement, and higher status than was available in the past. Reduced promotion prospects have been accompanied by fewer permanent contracts
25 of employment and more part-time and fixed-term contracts. Such changes in employment prospects mean that employees either adapt their idea of what constitutes a career or become dissatisfied when their career expectations are not met.

C ___ Career crisis can result from such mismatches, or when work and home lives are in series conflict, or when the individual's job does not suit his or her abilities and personality. A severe career crisis will often lead to job change, and if the individual does
35 not manage the crisis proactively, it can result in damaging psychological experiences such as long-term depression, 'burn-out', or inability to hold down a job for a reasonable length of time.

D ___ In the mid-1990s, Herriot and Pemberton claimed
40 that the very notion of career had fundamentally changed because the bargain between employer and employee that held in the 1960s and 1970s no longer applied. Their research was concerned with managerial careers, although many of their points about the changing
45 employment relationship apply to all employees in organizations where a contractual guarantee of lifelong employment and job security is no longer the norm. The authors say that the old deal has changed to a new deal.

E ___ Loyalty and organizational commitment were
50 high wherever this trust existed, to the extent that each party would go the extra mile, even when there was no extrinsic benefit to be had. For example, in the banking industry, it was not unknown for employers

to help the families of loyal, long-serving employees
55 who died suddenly by paying out a greater financial benefit than they were contractually obliged to render. Employees who were approaching retirement or who underperformed for significant periods of time would be accommodated and tolerated rather than
60 summarily dismissed. People usually entered at the bottom and stayed with the organization throughout their careers, in general older people were not asked to leave.

F ___ Management style in the public sector has changed
65 towards giving greater significance to value for money and towards facilitating private company services. Professionals in both the public and private sectors are expected to be more 'businesslike' when dealing with clients. In industrial research and development,
70 employment for technicians and scientists has generally become less secure as employers frequently replace experienced employees as they reach middle age with younger people. The new deal as proposed by Herriot and Pemberton, is a much more transactional
75 relationship whereby each party weighs up the opportunities and costs of being in the relationship, adopting a short-term and less trusting attitude. The new deal is a less permanent psychological contract in which the two parties are unsure about what is being
80 offered and what will be offered in the future. The new deal, Herriot and Pemberton surmise, is a less happy relationship than the old.

Old deal

You offered	Organization offered
Loyalty – not leaving	Security of employment
Conformity – doing what you were asked	Promotional prospects
Commitment – going the extra mile	Training and development
Trust – they'll keep their promises	Care in trouble

New deal

You offer	Organization offers
Long hours	High pay
Added responsibility	Rewards for performance
Broader skills	A job
Tolerance of change and ambiguity	

Source: Pinnington & Edwards *Introduction to Human Resource Management*, Oxford University Press, 2000

Glossary

blue collar (page 9): manual work, as opposed to white collar clerical and managerial work

extrinsic (line 52): outside/external

proactive(ly) (line 35): taking charge of a situation by making things happen rather than waiting for them to happen

render (line 56): give (legal)

C | Critical evaluation

Discuss these questions.

- How widespread do you think the 'old deal' described in the text really was?
- How far does this old deal/new deal description apply to your country or region? Is there, for instance, a division between the public and private sectors or between more traditional and modern industries?
- In your opinion, what are the advantages and drawbacks of the new and old deal?

Business vocabulary

A | Key notions: reducing and simplifying

1 **Match the words in *italics* in 1–6 to the definitions a–f.**

1 Since they *streamlined* the recruitment process they are able to take on new staff more quickly. ___
2 Following privatization they *de-layered* the organization by cutting several grades in middle management. ___
3 Head office has been systematically *eroding* the responsibility and discretion of provincial managers. ___
4 Sub-contracting some functions has allowed us to *trim* the workforce with little noticeable impact on our service. ___
5 They decided to *scale back* their US network to more manageable levels. ___
6 In the current economic climate a lot of companies are choosing to *downsize* their workforce. ___

a reduce the volume, level of activity
b reduce the number of people working in an organization
c reduce the number of stages needed to do something to make it more efficient
d reduce without having too great an impact
e reduce the levels in an organization's hierarchy
f reduce and weaken by slowly wearing it away

2 **Read the employees' comments on changes at work. What has happened and how do you think they feel about it? Use words from 1.**

1 They expect us to be loyal to the company, but then every month it seems as though our conditions get a little bit worse every year.
What has happened?

_____

How do you think they feel about it?

_____

2 It was a real shock, one day I went into work and I found out that I no longer had a job, my grade no longer existed! And with it my company car and pension.
What has happened?

_____

How do you think they feel about it?

_____

3 Nearly everybody goes through a difficult time during their working lives. One day, my firm decided it needed to lose 300 people and I was one of them. They said they wanted to be 'leaner and meaner'. What has happened?

_____

How do you think they feel about it?

_____

4 They cut a couple of people in reception and another one in sales and marketing in order to cut costs. They say that it won't make a difference, but I'm not so sure. What has happened?

_____

How do you think they feel about it?

_____

5 Since they introduced a self-service system in the canteen people don't have to waste so much time. What has happened?

_____

How do you think they feel about it?

_____

B | Career collocations

1 The text on page 10 contains a number of collocations (typical combinations of words). Look back at the text and find more collocations with the words below.

2 What other words can you think of that collocate with these items?

satisfaction

C | Personal qualities

1 Complete the definitions by matching 1–6 to a–f.

1 If you are upwardly mobile ... ___
2 If you are willing to go the extra mile ... ___
3 If you are suffering from burn-out ... ___
4 If you fulfil your side of the bargain ... ___
5 If you are able to hold down a job ... ___
6 If you are tolerant of change ... ___

a you respect what you agreed to do, and carry it out.
b you are moving to a higher, richer, social position.
c you easily accept new situations and ways of doing things.
d you are prepared to do more than what is usually expected to achieve your goal.
e your job has exhausted you mentally, physically, or both.
f you show that you are capable of sustained work over a period.

2 Study the short extracts from emails, letters and job advertisements. What kind of person are they describing? Use the expressions from 1.

1 In accordance with our agreement I paid all the fees in advance; however when I arrived on the first day of the course I discovered that there was not in fact a class at my level.

_____

2 Despite a chequered employment record we have been pleasantly surprised and impressed by her determination to turn up for work every day in the last six months and her good time-keeping.

_____

3 I was sorry to hear how tough things are for you at the moment. I think you should take a long holiday and maybe try something entirely different for a while. This might help you to find some of your old enthusiasm for the job.

_____

4 The ideal candidate will be a goal-motivated individual ready to do whatever is required to satisfy his customers.

_____

5 Thank you for your letter concerning xxxxxxxxx. I am afraid I am unable to lend my unqualified support for this candidate as in our experience he found it hard to cope with adjustments to his working schedule and the introduction of new technology.

_____

6 His grandfather was a simple peasant farmer while both parents were primary school teachers. It is extraordinary that from this background he went on to be a successful businessman and TV personality.

_____

Writing skills

Writing topic sentences

Well-constructed paragraphs often begin with a sentence that introduces its topic.

Example (paragraph E from text on page 10):

The old deal was a relational contract whereby each party – employer and employee – learnt to trust one another over time.

1 **Study the three opening paragraph sentences. Say what you think the rest of the paragraph will discuss.**

  1 There is little doubt that profound changes took place in British IR (Industrial Relations) in the 1980s.
  2 Organizational culture establishes norms and expectations of how people should be treated and serves the needs of the organization.
  3 Victor Vroom's book *Work and Motivation* is regarded by many as a landmark in the field of motivation.

2 **Read the short essay that discusses the evolution of different recruitment methods. Expand the notes to create introductory topic sentences for paragraphs B and C.**

  people – generally accepted most important part of an organization

  Example:

  It is generally accepted that the most important part of any organization is its people.

  Success or failure depends on how it attracts, exploits and retains this human capital. Yet for much of the time, staff selection can be a hit or miss affair. And as we are aware, the wrong choice can be damaging for the person who has been recruited in error. There is much debate about how far recruiting candidates for a new post is an art or a science.

  recent years orgs trying to make process more scientific

  B _____

  _____

  They take care to establish the key competencies they are seeking for particular roles. Recruiters have come to realize that they should not focus on recruiting the best or the most ambitious candidates, but the most suitable and the best 'fit' for the role in question. After all, a frequent complaint is that somebody left after a few weeks or months because they felt 'over-qualified' for a post.

  large orgs use psychologists/psychometric tests to help with choice

  C _____

  _____

  These psychometric tests fall into two main groups: those that assess reasoning skills, and those that seek to uncover personality traits. Of course, the value of these tests rests on how well they are able to predict future performance. Organizations may not always feel competent to carry out selection procedures themselves and turn to outside agencies and assessment centres.

3 **Write your own topic sentence for paragraph D.**

  D _____

  _____

  It is interesting to note that gender differences come into play here with female graduates being able to predict their own performance far more accurately than their male counterparts. It would appear that female candidates are more aware of their own strengths and weaknesses.

4 **Write the concluding paragraph by expanding the notes.**

  critics don't like face to face interviews – but quick and easy. Can we work together – yes/no? Drawback – interviewers recruit people like them!

  _____

  _____

  _____

  _____

  _____

  _____

  _____

  _____

  _____

Research task

Select a major listed company and find out as much as you can about their graduate recruitment programme. Compare this with how graduates are recruited to the civil service in your country. What are the differences in terms of conditions and career paths?

3 Renewing the organization

Study focus

1 Look at the diagram on the next page. How closely does it match your own experience of how people deal with change?

Reading strategies

A | Identifying main and supporting ideas

1 Read the text. Which paragraph deals with/ summarizes these main ideas?

1 Changing parts of an organization whilst maintaining the existing structure and fundamental beliefs. ___
2 Change within an organization is inevitable and necessary. It must be well coordinated and managed. ___
3 A practical example of handling change in two different work cultures. ___
4 Companies coping with change across different countries. ___
5 A complete shift in the organization – in the ways things are done, or in the fundamental beliefs of the organization. ___

2 Read paragraph B again. Find examples of these supporting ideas:

1 examples
2 extra details
3 more explanation

3 Read the rest of the text again and find supporting ideas in each paragraph. What techniques does the writer use to support his ideas?

B | Reading for detailed understanding

Choose the correct option for each paragraph.

Paragraph A

1 According to the author ...
a firms should question if change is absolutely necessary.
b change needs to occur in response to outside factors.
c sometimes changes here and there are the best way to deal with problems.
d transformational change can be achieved in a series of small steps.

Paragraph B

2 Which is *not* mentioned as a problem of introducing strategic change across MNCs?
a Linguistic problems that may cause unintended misunderstandings.
b Different cultures having different perceptions of change.
c Change may appear unnecessary where subsidiaries enjoy local protection.
d Different managerial practices and accepted forms of working may hinder change.

Paragraph C

3 What does the author say about incremental change?
a It is the exclusive prerogative of managers.
b Organizational beliefs can be shaken by incremental change too.
c It may provoke surprising levels of resistance.
d Managers may approve subordinates' suggestions for change.

Paragraph D

4 According to the author, how are leaders viewed in most European countries?
a The success of a leader's firm depends on his/her vision.
b Leaders are there to make the most of the firm's attributes.
c Leaders are the masters of compromise and promote company harmony.
d Leaders are there to evaluate the opportunities they are presented with.

Paragraph E

5 What does the Lucas Car Braking case study seem to show?
a German plants needed the shock provided by transformational change.
b Both plants eventually adopted the same change strategy.
c Change needed to be handled quite differently in each location.
d Incremental change can never result in transformational change.

Global management of change

A All types of firm, multinationals or single-country, small or large, single business or diversified, need constantly to undertake operational renewal in order to renew those parts of the organization that are ageing. However, for change to succeed it must be coordinated throughout the
5 firm. Piecemeal change may create new problems without solving the old ones. Also, due to the inherent instability in the business environment today, firms often find themselves facing the need to undertake strategic renewal in order to pursue a change strategy and/or to adjust to changing environmental factors. Where environmental change is slow and/or small,
10 organizational change is likely to be in small, incremental steps. The changes that the organization needs to undertake are likely to be larger, however, where the environmental changes are larger or because it wishes to change its strategy significantly. Such changes are transformational.

B Strategic change in multinationals is more complex than that in single-
15 country firms. The more complex the environment within which change takes place, the more difficult it is to design and implement a coherent change strategy. Multinational firms are companies that operate across several countries, which creates a complex and sometimes chaotic *mélange* of management practices influenced by different national cultures
20 and institutions. In addition, some subsidiaries are more aware of the competitive nature of the business environment, perhaps because the subsidiary or the industry is protected or subsidized by the government, and hence may not understand the importance of change and may resist it. Further, people's attitudes towards change are also affected by a set of
25 culture-specific factors, such as taken-for-granted behaviour, norms and values, which adds another layer of complexity to change management in multinational firms. The different behaviours and attitudes of employees and management at subsidiary level towards change increase the potential for conflict between the centre and subsidiaries, and may hinder the
30 success of the change strategy (Andrews and Chompusri 2001).

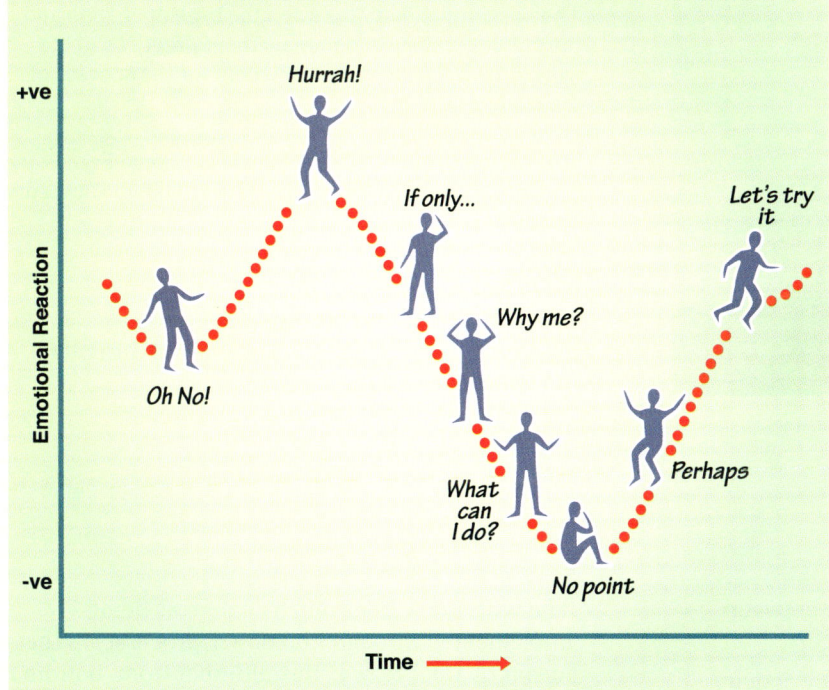

Types of change

Organizations have to be prepared to undertake both incremental change and transformational change.

Incremental change

C By far the most frequent sort
35 of change in organizations is incremental change. Incremental change alters behaviours in the organization, but generally leaves undisturbed the more deeply held
40 organizational beliefs. Examples of incremental change aim to produce more 'of something' and/or do things better. The incorporation of an export department into
45 the existing domestic marketing function when a firm begins exporting would probably be considered incremental, since no large-scale changes are involved.
50 Incremental change is a role for management. Managers deal with the physical resources of an organization – with its capital, raw materials, technology and
55 the demonstrable skills of their workforce. They are concerned with efficiency and with mastering routines. They are the people who resolve issues as they arise:
60 they do things right – working within defined policies. However, although incremental change may be sanctioned by managers, much incremental change is originated
65 by the people most intimately connected with the organization's processes, its products/services and its customers. If they are suitably empowered, they can
70 bring about the required change themselves. Incremental change is more associated with management rather than leadership, since management generally continues
75 current activities with a concern for efficiency. Incremental change does not lead to a change in the implicit fundamental beliefs underpinning the organization's
80 way of working.

Transformational change

D Transformational change involves changing one
or more of the fundamental organizational beliefs,
and with it the values of the organization. Examples
of transformational change are the changes in the
85 processes of doing things very differently, or with
undertaking very different activities. In such cases
management alone generally is not sufficient – what
is required is leadership. Leaders are people who are
concerned with effectiveness: they do the right things,
90 they make policy. They act on the emotional and
spiritual resources of the organization dealing with
its values, commitment, and aspirations (Bennis and
Nanus 1985:21). Leaders are also issue *finders*: they
seek issues in their search for opportunities. Zalenik
95 (1992:129, 131) distinguishes between managers and
leaders: 'Managers aim to shift balances of power
towards solutions acceptable as compromises among
conflicting values, [while] leaders develop fresh ideas

to long-standing problems and open issues to new
100 options.' But the way in which leadership is viewed
differs between countries. Kay (1995:15) makes an
interesting contrast between US and UK views on
leadership and those of the rest of Europe. In the
US and UK (and to some extent France) the chief
105 executive is seen as the master of the organization and
business success becomes, in effect, realizing the chief
executive's vision. In Japan and most of the rest of
Europe, senior executives are seen as the servants of
the organization, and success is seen as maximizing the
110 value of an organization's distinctive capabilities.

Types of change and national cultures

E While all types of strategic change, small or large,
incremental or radical, are to a varying degree difficult
to manage, strategic change in multinational firms
is much more difficult to manage than change in
115 firms operating in a single country. This is because
employees and management in different countries hold
different managerial values and adhere to different
managerial practices. Harding's (1996:111) study of
strategic change of Lucas Car Braking systems in
120 Britain and Germany found that during the process of
change, the British workforce were stuck in what he
called the 'bad practices learning phase'; in contrast
the German workforce were more receptive to learning
in the post-shock phase. As a result, management
125 used a different method of change in the two sites.
In the case of the British workforce, Harding argues
that to overcome the inherent resistance to change
there is a need for a shock or a transformational
change. In contrast, the German workforce's
130 acceptance of the need for change makes the gradual
or incremental change strategy more appropriate.
That is, compatibility between the type of change and
the cultural values and management practices of the
workforce is a necessary ingredient for the success of
135 the change strategy.

Source: Chapter 11 of Kamel Melahi, J George Frynas and
Paul Finlay *Global Strategic Management*, Oxford University
Press 2006

Glossary

adhere to (line 117): to follow/believe in
coherent (line 16): logical and well-organized; easy to
    understand

C | Critical evaluation

Discuss these questions.

- In your view, how clear is the difference between
incremental and transformational change?
- If leaders begin as managers, how do they acquire
the skills they need to become leaders?

- The writer describes much change as being
implemented through 'top down' processes. What is
meant by this? How is this different from 'bottom up'
change?

Business vocabulary

A | Organizational change

1 Match words 1–10 to definitions a–j.

1 sanction ___
2 empower ___
3 inherent ___
4 incorporate ___
5 underpin ___
6 overcome ___
7 hinder ___
8 piecemeal ___
9 incremental ___
10 undertake ___

a to succeed in dealing with a problem that prevented you from achieving something
b gradual, developing little by little
c to make it difficult for someone to do something
d done at different times and in different ways rather than logically and carefully
e to give someone the tools and authority to do something
f to provide essential support
g to make yourself responsible for something and start to do it
h formally give permission
i to include something so that it forms part of something else/sth bigger
j that is a basic part of something and cannot be removed

2 Complete the sentences using the words from 1. Make any necessary changes.

1 When they decided to _____ accounts within the marketing department they had not taken the differences in departmental cultures into consideration.
2 After much discussion, the board _____ moving production overseas.
3 _____ adjustments are rarely a substitute for full-scale reform.
4 They _____ the changes without taking into account the international repercussions.
5 An _____ problem with introducing change is that conservative elements will always oppose it.
6 Progress has been _____ by a lack of support from older managers.
7 They need to _____ their mutual suspicion if they are going to make progress.
8 There are two basic types of change: radical change and _____ change.
9 For all their talk of _____ workers, decisions continued to be made by senior management.
10 The previous production system was _____ by a cheap and ready supply of raw materials from its overseas colonies.

B | Verbs with over-, under-

Complete the sentences by using over- or under- to form an entire word.

1 In exit interviews, the two most commonly cited reasons for resignations were being _____ valued and _____ paid.
2 High employee protection led to businesses relying on _____ time and short-term contracts rather than the creation of permanent posts.
3 After the takeover there was an _____ lying mistrust towards the parent company.
4 During the 'old deal', when employees felt _____ due for promotion it was possible to move them up a grade.
5 In the 1990s the firm _____ hauled its recruitment policy in its efforts to reduce staff turnover.
6 Unions were obliged to give an _____ taking on the provision of a minimum service.
7 Before examining our future human resources needs, we should first have an _____ view of our current staffing structure.
8 A common way for organizations to reduce their _____ heads is by subcontracting non-core services.
9 The agreement was _____ written by the principal service providers.
10 It was not a deliberate decision; it was the result of a simple _____ sight.

C | Opposite meanings

1 Study the words and the definitions. One of these appears in the text on page 15. Re-phrase sentences 1–6 using the appropriate word.

1 oversight
   a a mistake caused by forgetting to do something [C]
   b responsibility for supervision [U]

2 sanction
   a to punish
   b to approve

3 table
   a to propose a topic for discussion (UK)
   b to put a subject to one side (USA)

1 The CEO said there no immediate plans for discussing the suggestions.

_____

2 It wasn't deliberate. A careless clerk simply put a number in the wrong column.

_____

3 A new system of fines has been introduced for people who fail to submit their tax returns on time.

_____

4 Angry shareholders are going to pass a motion requesting an explanation on low dividends at the next annual general meeting.

_____

5 The multi-billion dollar project has finally received the green light.

_____

6 A committee of experts has been appointed to monitor deep water drilling activities.

_____

2 Read what the people say. What misunderstanding has taken place?

1 I've never been so embarrassed in my life. I thought the board of directors wanted me to talk about my proposal in more detail, but when I started to they said they would hear it at a later date. I'm confused!

2 I was talking about having overall responsibility for the scheme, and they thought someone had forgotten to do something. We were speaking completely at cross-purposes.

3 So do they want to stop the project in its tracks, or do they want it to go ahead? I'm not at all clear what they want.

Writing skills

A | Paragraph features

There are a number of features that are common to paragraphs. Not all of these features are in every paragraph but at least some will be. Nearly all paragraphs will contain a topic sentence and a variety of methods of support that are logically organized. There will also be a concluding comment or a transition to the next paragraph.

1 Look at the following paragraph features.

1 Which ones support the main idea?
2 Which come at the end of the paragraph?

   a provides a definition
   b gives a concluding comment
   c expresses a relationship
   d introduces the topic of the paragraph
   e develops the argument
   f provides a transition to the next paragraph

2 Look at paragraph B of the text on page 15. Identify the features from 1 in one or more sentences. One of the features is not included, which is it?

B | Paragraph structure

1 Look at the opening sentences in each example paragraph. Continue the paragraph by putting the remaining sentences in the most logical and appropriate order.

Paragraph 1
Opening sentence: It is often said that change occurs because the time for an idea has come.

a This 'change master' will be an indefatigable campaigner for the idea in question and will encourage, inspire and cajole others into following his or her lead. ___

b Without such an ambassador change initiatives can quickly run of steam and be forgotten. ___

c Yet, whatever the merits of a good idea, change always needs a champion to see it through. ___

d All this goes to explain why ideas that may look good on paper never gain the momentum to make them succeed in practice. ___

e This is usually not enough overcome the inertia of people who fail to recognize the advantages of change, nor the antagonism of vested interests that will fight change at all cost. ___

Paragraph 2

Opening sentence: Observers have noted that the way people respond to organization change follows a remarkably similar pattern.

a This risks turning into despondency as the individual no longer feels in control of his own destiny and sinks into depression. ___

b This is swiftly followed by a feeling of elation that something new is about to happen. ___

c The first reaction seems to be one of shock as the news sinks in. ___

d Finally, the individual adopts the change and participates in it willingly, at which point the pattern is complete. ___

e Fortunately, most people are able to pull themselves out of this and gradually come around to the acceptance of change and the advantages that it might bring. ___

f However, this is rapidly replaced by a fuller contemplation of the upset that change means for the individual. ___

2 **Read this essay title. This student has planned three main paragraphs on the question. Expand the notes for each topic into full paragraphs. Use the features from A1 as necessary.**

One of the biggest challenges family businesses face is how to effectively manage inter-generational succession. What issues and problems arise from this type of change?

Paragraph 1 – problems with the founder

- *Succession handovers/difficult in family firms.*
- *Family firms under control of founding member.*
- *Jealously, family members want a say in business/interference.*

_____

_____

_____

_____

_____

_____

Paragraph 2 – challenges the successor faces

- *Inexperienced successor has more problems with other family members and staff.*
- *Successor has expectations/plans different from founding member.*
- *Employees may not respect abilities and experience of successor.*

_____

_____

_____

_____

_____

Paragraph 3 – ways to deal with the problems

- *Good idea for successor to gain experience outside company.*
- *Succession needs careful handling.*
- *If no worthy successor appoint an outsider.*

_____

_____

_____

_____

_____

_____

3 **Compare your paragraphs with a partner. Which features from A1 has your partner used?**

4 **The student decides to add an additional paragraph before paragraph 1 with the following topic.**

What is change and why is it difficult?

1 Use your own ideas and the reading text to develop a paragraph on this topic.

2 Compare your paragraph with a partner. Identify the features from A1 in their paragraph.

Research task

Research one of these topics.

1 The Japanese vehicle manufacturer, Nissan, was taken over by French car-maker Renault. Find out what changes occurred as a result, and what impact this has had on traditional Japanese management practices.

2 How far were cultural differences responsible for the failure of the merger between the German car manufacturer Daimler, and the US car-maker Chrysler?

4 Ensuring good behaviour

Study focus

1 Imagine that you have a large sum of money to invest in major companies. What research will you carry out before deciding where to place your money?

2 Read the definitions and discuss …

   a how they are connected.
   b how they should protect investors from unexpected risks.

> **audit:** (Accounting) An official examination of business and financial records to see that they are true and correct.

> **corporate governance:** The way in which directors and managers control a company and make decisions, especially decisions that have an important effect on shareholders.

(Definitions taken from the *Oxford Business English Dictionary for learners of English*)

Reading strategies

A | Using background knowledge to understand content

1 Answer the questions.

   1 Can you think of any recent financial scandals or company failures that have resulted from poor corporate governance or inaccurate audits?
   2 What do you know about the Enron scandal? What was the cause and result? Make notes.
   3 What do you know about the Barings scandal? What was the cause and result? Make notes.

2 Read the text and compare your notes to the information given.

B | Reading for general understanding

Tick the answer/s that are the most appropriate.

Introductory paragraphs A–C focus on …
   a how businesses need both internal and external controls.
   b the damage caused when businesses collapse.
   c the necessity for clear and honest financial reporting.
   d how poor decisions may lead to the failure of businesses.

C | Reading for detailed understanding

1 Read the introduction again and make questions for the answers.

   Example:
   Question: *Why do companies need investors?*
   Answer: Because without the funds they provide, they wouldn't be able to grow.

   1 Question: _____
   Answer: Well, they can look at the company's accounts and other available information.
   2 Question: _____
   Answer: Because they have been checked by an outside auditor.
   3 Question: _____
   Answer: Not entirely, certain aspects of the business aren't dealt with.
   4 Question: _____
   Answer: Everyone, from investors and employees, to suppliers and the community at large.
   5 Question: _____
   Answer: Effective corporate governance.

2 Read the paragraphs about Barings bank and Enron again. Choose which sentences 1–8 refer to Barings or Enron.

   Which institution … ?
   1 was one of the US's biggest companies
   Barings ____   Enron ____
   2 became the victim of one man's risk-taking
   Barings ____   Enron ____
   3 was badly affected by a natural disaster
   Barings ____   Enron ____
   4 created financial instruments to hide its losses
   Barings ____   Enron ____
   5 was sold for a symbolic sum
   Barings ____   Enron ____
   6 had inadequate supervision of individual employees
   Barings ____   Enron ____
   7 exploited the weakness of its auditors
   Barings ____   Enron ____
   8 was eventually denounced by an honest employee
   Barings ____   Enron ____

3 What lessons should the business learn from Barings and Enron?

Corporate governance

A Businesses around the world need to be able to attract funding from investors in order to expand and grow. Before investors decide to invest their funds in a particular business, they will want to be as sure as
5 they can that the business is financially sound and will continue to be so in the foreseeable future. Investors therefore need to have confidence that the business is being well managed and will continue to be profitable.

B In order to have this assurance, investors look to the
10 published annual report and accounts of the business and to other information releases that the company might make. They expect that the annual report and accounts will represent a true picture of the company's present position – after all, the annual report and
15 accounts are subject to an annual audit whereby an independent external auditor examines the business' records and transactions, and certifies that the annual report and accounts have been prepared in accordance with accepted accounting standards and give a 'true
20 and fair view' of the business' activities. However, although the annual report may give a reasonably accurate picture of the business' activities and financial position at that point in time, there are many facets of the business that are not effectively reflected in the
25 annual report and accounts.

C There have been a number of high-profile corporate collapses that have arisen despite the fact that the annual report and accounts seemed fine. These corporate collapses have had an adverse effect on
30 many people: shareholders who have seen their investment reduced to nothing; employees who have lost their jobs and, in many cases, the security of their company pension, which has also evaporated overnight; suppliers of goods and services to the failed
35 companies; and the economic impact on the local and international communities in which the failed companies operated. In essence, corporate collapses affect us all. Why have such collapses occurred? What might be done to prevent such collapses happening
40 again? How can investor confidence be restored? The answers to these questions are all linked to corporate governance: a lack of effective corporate governance meant that such collapses could occur; good corporate governance can help prevent such collapses
45 happening again and restore investor confidence. To illustrate why corporate failures might occur, despite the companies seeming healthy, it is helpful to review a few examples from recent years, each of which has sent shock waves through stock markets around the world.

D Barings Bank
50 The downfall in 1995 of one of England's oldest established banks was brought about by the actions of one man, Nick Leeson. In 1993, he was based in Singapore and made more than ten million pounds, about ten per cent of Barings' total profit that year.
55 However, his run of luck was not to last and, when a severe earthquake in Japan affected the stock market adversely he incurred huge losses of Barings' money. He requested more funds from Barings' head office in London, which were sent to him, but unfortunately he
60 suffered further losses. The losses were so great, 850 million pounds, that Barings bank collapsed and was eventually bought for one pound by ING, the Dutch banking and insurance group. Barings Bank has been criticized for its lack of effective internal controls at
65 that time, which left Nick Leeson able to cover up the

losses he was making for quite a number of months. The case also illustrates the importance of having effective supervision, by experienced staff with a good understanding of the processes and procedures, of staff
70 who are able to expose the company to such financial disaster. The collapse of Barings Bank sent ripples across the world as the importance of effective internal controls and appropriate monitoring was reinforced.

E Enron

Enron was ranked in the USA's Fortune top ten list of
75 companies, based on its turnover in 2000. Its published accounts for the year ended 31 December 2000 showed a seemingly healthy profit of US$979 million and there was nothing obvious to alert shareholders to the impending disaster that was going to unfold over the
80 next year or so, making Enron the largest bankruptcy in US history.

F Enron's difficulties related to its activities in the energy market and the setting up of a series of 'special purpose entities' (SPEs). Enron used the SPEs to conceal large
85 losses from the market by giving the impression that key exposures were hedged (covered) by third parties. However the SPEs were really nothing more than an extension of Enron itself and so Enron's risks were not covered. Some of the SPEs were used to transfer
90 funds to some of Enron's directors. In October 2001, Enron declared a non-recurring loss of US$1billion and also had to disclose a US$1.2 billion write-off against shareholders' funds. It looked as though a takeover might be on the cards from a rival, Dynergy,
95 but in November, announcements by Enron of further debts led to the takeover bid falling through, and in December 2001, Enron filed for bankruptcy.

G In retrospect, it seems that the directors were not questioned closely enough about the use of SPEs and
100 their accounting treatment. What has become clear is that there was some concern among Enron's auditors – Andersen – about the SPEs, and Enron's activities. Unfortunately Andersen failed to question the directors

hard enough and Andersen's own fate was sealed when
105 some of its employees shredded paperwork relating to Enron, thus obliterating vital evidence and contributing to the demise of Andersen which has itself been taken over by various rivals.

H Interestingly, one of the employees at Enron, Sherron
110 Watkins had made her concerns known to the chief finance officer, and Arthur Andersen as early as 1996. In 2001 she became aware that an extensive fraud was taking place with SPEs being used as a vehicle to hide Enron's growing losses. She became the whistleblower to
115 one of the most infamous corporate scandals of all time.

I The Enron case highlights the overriding need for integrity in business: for the directors to act with integrity and honesty, and for the external audit firms to be able to ask searching questions of the directors
120 without holding back for fear of offending a lucrative client. Enron also highlights the need for independent non-executive directors who are experienced enough to be able to ask searching questions in board and committee meetings to try to ensure that the business
125 is operated appropriately.

···

Source: Christine Mallin *Corporate Governance*, Oxford University Press, 2010

Glossary

adverse (line 29): negative, unpleasant, or harmful

facet (line 23): aspect of something

foreseeable future (line 6): not very distant future time

impending (line 79): likely to happen very soon

in retrospect (line 98): used when we look back on a past event or situation and then change our opinion

obliterate (line 106): destroy completely

reinforce (line 73): to make something stronger

ripples (line 71): the concentric rings caused by dropping an object into calm water

shred (line 105): cut paper into fine pieces so they can no longer be read

D | Reading for inference

Read the text again and answer the questions.

1 Why do you think Nick Leeson was given such a free hand with his investments?

2 How could an earthquake have caused Leeson to have made such catastrophic losses?

3 What do you think was the critical 'point of no return' for Barings?

4 Why do you think Leeson's supervision by senior staff was so ineffective?

5 Who at Enron do you think was responsible for the misleading set of accounts for the year ended 2000?

6 Does the writer think that Enron's SPEs were set up in good faith?

7 What do you think the relationship between Enron and its auditors Andersen was like?

8 Why do you think nobody wanted to listen to Sherron Watkins?

E | Note-taking

Make notes on the similarities and differences between the Barings Bank scandal and the Enron affair. Consider ...

- The people involved
- Who knew what
- The time span
- Warning signals
- Supervision and governance

F | Critical evaluation

Discuss these questions.

- How could senior management at Barings Bank have prevented the collapse?
- Why do you think people chose to ignore the earlier warnings of the Enron 'whistleblower'?
- How dangerous is it to 'blow the whistle' on your own organization's activities?
- How can the following people keep a company honest?
  – The CEO/MD and his/her management team
  – The board of directors and its chairman
  – Non-executive directors
  – Major shareholders and other investors
  – Employees and other stakeholders

Business vocabulary

A | Company finance

1 Solve the anagrams to produce the word that goes with each definition.

1 ADRUTIO

_____: a person or business that officially examines the financial and business records of a company

2 OLCASPLE

_____: fall down suddenly

3 ORBDA

_____: the group of people chosen by investors in a company to control a company and appoint its senior officers

4 ROPXESUE

_____: the amount of money that is open to risk/ being lost

5 EHDEG

_____: to protect yourself against the risk of losing money in the future

6 NTGIEYRIT

_____: the quality of being honest and having string moral principles

7 TCURLVAIE

_____: producing large amounts of money

8 OSNDU

_____: stable and in good condition

9 HRAESOSHLERD

_____: people who own units of a company

10 HILTWSEBELROW

_____: a person who informs the authorities that the company they work for is doing something wrong

11 KTEAOEVR/IBD

_____: an attempt to take control of a company by acquiring a majority of its shares

12 AKNBYPCRTU

_____: the state of not having enough money to pay what you owe

2 Complete the passage using the words from 1.

Companies are required to produce an annual set of accounts that have been certified by an external ¹_____ as being a true reflection of the state of the company. Naturally, these outside experts should be truly independent and simply not scared of losing a ²_____ contract. These financial documents should demonstrate how ³_____ a firm is, and show, for instance, whether it is making a healthy profit or heading for the rocks of ⁴_____! In either case, this may make the business a worthwhile target for a ⁵_____. Wise investors, of course, ⁶_____ against risk by spreading their investments around; thus reducing their overall ⁷_____ should one firm fail. Ultimately, much depends on the honesty and ⁸_____ of the CEO and the ⁹_____ of directors at the heart of a firm's governance. Otherwise, by the time a ¹⁰_____ is ready to risk his career by raising the alarm it can be too late for ¹¹_____ to rescue their money or to save the firm from a sudden and unexpected ¹²_____.

B | Phrasal verbs for corporate governance

1 Match 1–10 to a–j to form sentences.

1 They destroyed documents to *cover* ___
2 The proposed share issue has *fallen* ___
3 This isn't the time to *hold* ___
4 The company's failure was *brought* ___
5 We'll just have to *write* the debt ___
6 They need to *set* ___
7 Dishonest people can usually *get* ___
8 They hoped other banks would *bail* ___
9 They were forced to *file* ___
10 It took them years to *sort* ___

a *them out*, but they were wrong.
b *up* their wrong doing.
c *about* by unwise expansion.
d *around* rules and regulations.
e *out* their accounts and crooked dealings.
f *back*, decisive action is required.
g *for* bankruptcy when the scandal broke.
h *off* – we'll never get our money back.
i *up* effective procedures for governance.
j *through*, we can't find an underwriter.

2 Decide which synonyms belong with which of the phrasal verbs in *italics* in 1.

cause	establish	fail to happen
submit a request	conceal the truth	cancel
wait and see	avoid	rescue
restore order		

3 Imagine that you are a journalist for a TV channel specializing in business news. You have just heard that auditors have discovered evidence of malpractice at HBN Holdings, a huge property developer. A senior employee has also spoken out against the company. Invent a short news report that uses some of the phrasal verbs and key terms.

Writing skills

A | Connecting and contrasting ideas

1 Sort the words of similar meaning under headings 1–4.

results in	likewise	because
although	since	similarly
in addition	hence	contributes to
furthermore	despite	while
consequently	leads to	nevertheless
besides	whereas	therefore
due to	moreover	thus
however	conversely	even though

1	2	3	4
Contrast	Related examples	Cause and effect	Similarities

24

2 Choose the correct option.

1 Leeson was a star trader, *moreover/nevertheless* he was considered the firm's golden boy.
At one point he made ten per cent of Barings' annual profit, *despite/however* his luck eventually ran out and he started to lose big time.

2 He tried to cover up his losses by gambling even more heavily, *thus/likewise* getting deeper and deeper into trouble.

3 Nick Leeson was sentenced to a term of imprisonment; Enron CEO Jeffrey Skilling was *likewise/moreover*. *However/In addition,* the latter was given a much longer sentence.

4 *Despite/However* her repeated warnings nobody heeded Sherron Watkins, *thus/similarly* when action was finally taken it was too late to rescue Enron.

5 Poor corporate governance eventually *results in/due to* a financial crisis at the heart of the organization.

3 Complete the sentences using the words from 1.

1 Several Enron directors were taken to court, _____ they managed to escape punishment by parting with huge sums of their personal wealth.

2 The Barings and Enron scandals sent shock waves through the financial community, _____ demonstrating the need for rigorous corporate governance.

3 Arthur Andersen's reputation was badly damaged by the Enron scandal, _____ its eventual collapse came as no surprise.

4 _____ senior executives must have suspected what was going on for years before the scandal broke, in the interim they kept their heads in the sand.

5 _____ the problems of Barings bank could be attributed to one person, Enron was riddled with corruption and bad practice.

B | Writing practice

1 Study the notes about the Parmalat scandal. What similarities are there with the Barings Bank story, or the Enron scandal?

Parmalat

Italian firm – long-life milk

Founder: Calisto Tanzi

Expanded by buying other firms. A real success story.

In 2003 the firm couldn't make a bond payment.

Investors believed enough cash reserves. Untrue. Big losers small investors.

Using money from new investors to pay old investors

False accounting methods

Debts of 13 billion pounds

After 3-year trial Tanzi found guilty of falsifying accounts and misleading investors. 18 year sentence. Tanzi's art collection seized – not enough to pay back small investors.

2 Now use the notes to create a paragraph about the Parmalat scandal. Make sure you include some of the ways of connecting and contrasting ideas.

_____

_____

_____

_____

_____

_____

Research task

Choose two of the companies listed below. Find out how they became involved in a company collapse or financial scandal.

- Royal Ahold – a Dutch retail group and the world's third largest food retailer
- China Aviation Oil
- Satyam – an Indian computer services company
- HIH – an Australian insurance company
- Royal Bank of Scotland

5 Motivation

Study focus

1 **Read about the Western Electric factory. How can the research process influence people's behaviour?**

The *Western Electric* factory based in Hawthorne near Chicago was the subject of a series of experiments conducted by Elton Mayo. He wanted to see if lighting levels at the factory had an impact on productivity. The study yielded some surprising results.

– When lighting levels were increased productivity went up.

– When lighting levels were lowered productivity went up as well.

However; when the studies finished productivity fell back to original levels.

2 **Researchers often talk about 'the Hawthorne Effect'. What do you think they mean by this?**

3 **Why is it a good idea to bear the Hawthorne Effect in mind when analysing the results of experimental studies and surveys?**

Reading strategies

A | Scanning for specific information

1 **Scan the text and find out what the following abbreviations stand for.**

MHT _____

JCM _____

JDS _____

GNS _____

2 **What names are associated with each theory or abbreviation?**

MHT _____

JCM _____

JDS _____

GNS _____

B | Reading and note-taking

Notes and tables can help us make sense of a complicated reading passage. Read the text and complete the following table with words and descriptions.

1 **MHT = motivator-hygiene theory**

motivator factors	hygiene factors
definition: _____	definition: _____
_____	_____
_____	_____
_____	_____
_____	_____

2 **JCM = job characteristics model**

core job characteristics   3 **psychological states**

1 ____ refers to _____
_____

2 ____ refers to _____   a _____
_____   _____

3 ____ refers to _____   b _____
_____   _____

4 ____ refers to _____   c _____
_____   _____

5 ____ refers to _____
_____

C | Reading for detailed understanding

Answer the questions.

1 According to Taylor, what was the best way of improving performance and efficiency?

2 What were some unforeseen consequences of the 'scientific management' approach?

3 What is the essential difference between motivator and hygiene factors? What examples does the writer give?

4 What weakness of Herzberg's theory does the writer point out?

5 Does JCM build on, or provide a radical alternative to Herzberg's theory?

6 What is the link between JCM's 'five core job characteristics', and its 'three critical psychological states'?

7 According to Hackman and Oldham, how do people with high GNS behave?

8 How far do the findings of the JDS support Hackman and Oldham's theories?

9 How clear is the importance of GNS on job motivation and performance?

Job design in historical perspective: an overview

A Frederick W. Taylor, who was the first to focus on job design for individuals, developed the 'scientific management' approach in 1911. Taylor's approach focused on specialization and simplification of jobs
5　as mechanisms to enhance efficiency and control performance. However, research has revealed that the routine and standardized tasks associated with the 'scientific management' approach have led to a number of unintended adverse consequences, such as
10　higher tardiness, lower motivation and productivity, and sabotage of work equipment. This meant that the gains made in the industrial engineering approach were often overshadowed by its negative effects. The problems associated with the industrial engineering
15　approach produced alternatives to job design. These new approaches focused on the motivation of employees at work as a key determinant of job attitude and performance. Two theories that have particularly affected the area of job design are the Motivator-
20　Hygiene Theory (MHT), which was developed by Frederick Herzberg and his colleagues in the 1960s, and the Job Characteristics Model (JCM), which was developed by Hackman and Oldham (1976, 1980) on the basis of earlier conceptual development by Turner and
25　Lawrence. The central theme of MHT is the distinction between motivator factors, which are intrinsic to the job itself (and include responsibility, achievement, recognition, and personal growth in competence), and hygiene factors, which are associated with the job
30　context or work setting (and include relationship with peers and subordinates, quality of supervision, base wage or salary, benefits and job security). According to MHT, while hygiene factors merely prevent job dissatisfaction, motivator factors increase workers'
35　motivation and satisfaction on the job.

B The theory in essence suggests that enriching employees' jobs, by adding responsibility, complexity and personal growth, is essential to increasing employee motivation and performance. Herzberg's
40　theory has inspired both research and several successful job design projects that provide evidence for the positive effect of motivator factors on individual and organizational outcomes. The theory, however, suffers from some weaknesses. These include the lack of
45　differentiation between factors, such as pay rises, that can serve both as hygiene and motivator factors; the lack of a suitable measurement instrument to assess the motivator and hygiene factors; and the failure of the theory to consider the effect of individual or cultural
50　differences on motivator and hygiene factors.

C The Job Characteristics model was developed by Hackman and Oldham in the 1970s and 1980s as an attempt to overcome some of the shortcomings of MHT. Specifically, the JCM focuses on five core
55　job characteristics: skill variety, task identity, task significance, autonomy and job feedback. Briefly, skill variety refers to the different number of skills needed to accomplish a job. Task identity focuses on whether the job requires completion for a whole, identifiable piece of
60　work. Task significance refers to the job's impact on the lives of other people in the organization or on society at large. Autonomy refers to the employee's level of freedom, independence, and discretion in determining how and when to do his or her job. Finally, job feedback
65　refers to the degree to which work activities provide the employee with direct and clear information about his or her job performance. According to the model, these five core characteristics affect three critical psychological states in turn: experienced meaningfulness of work,
70　experienced responsibility for work outcomes, and knowledge of work results. Skill variety, task identity and task significance are related to experienced meaningfulness, autonomy is related to experienced responsibility, and job feedback is related to knowledge
75　of results.

D These three psychological states in turn positively affect individual psychological and behavioural outcomes, namely high intrinsic work motivation, job performance, job satisfaction, and reduced
80 absenteeism and turnover. Finally, individual difference variables, which include growth need strength (GNS: the desire for learning and personal accomplishment at work), knowledge and skills, and context satisfaction (satisfaction with supervisors,
85 co-workers, income and job security), moderate the relationships among job characteristics, psychological states and the psychological and behavioural work outcomes. Specifically, according to the model, when individuals have high GNS (they strive to be involved
90 in challenging jobs), high knowledge and skills (they have the capabilities needed to accomplish the job successfully), and a high level of satisfaction with their supervisor, co-workers, pay and job security, they will respond well to enriched (challenging) jobs, because
95 they can pursue such jobs without distractions. On the other hand, if GNS and knowledge and skills are low, individuals will lack the motivation and ability to focus on and complete challenging jobs. In addition, if their level of satisfaction with their supervisors, co-workers,
100 pay and job security is low, they will be distracted and unable to focus on the job.

E To measure the model's variables and assess its validity, Hackman and Oldham developed the job diagnostic survey (JDS), which has subsequently been
105 widely used. In fact, most of the contemporary research on job design has drawn on the JCM. The results have found support for the major premises of the model. However, not all the theory's hypotheses have been equally supported. Specifically, there is strong
110 support, based on field experiments and cross sectional and longitudinal field surveys for the relationships between job characteristics and employee affective reactions (job satisfaction, growth satisfaction and internal motivation). Research results also support the
115 expected relationships between job characteristics and behavioural outcomes (performance and absenteeism). However, the magnitude of these associations is relatively weak. Research has also supported the mediating role of the psychological states, though
120 questions remain about the precise relationships between the particular job characteristics and the corresponding psychological states.

F Further, among the hypothesized moderators, GNS has been investigated the most, and the results are partially
125 supportive. A comprehensive study by Tiegs, Tetrick and Fried (1992) on a sample of nearly 7,000 individuals across different jobs and occupations failed to provide such support for moderating effects of GNS (as well as context satisfaction). However, reviews of the research
130 evidence by Fried and Ferris (1987), Loher et al (1985), Oldham, (1995) and Spector (1985), provide support for the moderating effect of GNS on the relationship between job characteristics and job satisfaction and performance. In addition there is little support for the
135 moderating effect of context satisfaction and there is little research on the moderating role of indicators of knowledge and skills. While the importance of job design to employee motivation and performance is well established, significant changes in the work
140 environment raise questions concerning job design in the twenty-first century.

Source: Cartwright and Cooper (ed.) *Oxford Handbook of Personnel Psychology*, Oxford University Press, 2008

Glossary

absenteeism (line 80): the fact of frequently being away from work

cross sectional survey (line 110): compares subjects at a point in time.

feedback (line 56): advice/information on performance

longitudinal survey (line 111): follows subjects over a period of time.

moderate (line 85): make something less severe

peers (line 31): colleagues at the same level

sabotage (line 11): the deliberate and malicious damage of equipment

shortcoming (line 53): fault/disadvantage

strive (line 89): work hard

D | Critical evaluation

Discuss these questions.

- Did the researchers we have read about need to put so much effort in uncovering what may be obvious, or common sense?

- What possible influence could the Hawthorne Effect have had on their research?

- How convinced are you by MHT and the JCM? What is their practical use in job design?

Business vocabulary

A | Performance and job satisfaction

1 **Find words in the text to match the definitions.**

   1 to make better/to improve/increase: _____
   2 part of the true nature of something: _____
   3 working alone/independently: _____
   4 to improve the quality of something: _____
   5 the act of not going to work: _____
   6 carry out/achieve (a job or task): _____
   7 ability to do something well: _____
   8 deliberate destruction or damage: _____
   9 negative effects: _____ _____

2 **Complete the sentences with a form of one of the words from 1.**

   1 Job satisfaction can be greatly _____ by offering a little more responsibility to the employee.
   2 The need to feel useful is _____ to the idea of job satisfaction in general.
   3 Managers found that when they allowed their staff to work more _____, and stopped micro-managing them, overall performance improved.
   4 If somebody is not _____ in their role, they will struggle to get any satisfaction from it.
   5 It is only possible to _____ a task if the working conditions are right.

3 **Rewrite these sentences using words from 1.**

   Example:

   If we don't address staff dissatisfaction, there will be negative effects.

   Failing to address staff dissatisfaction will have adverse consequences for the company.

   1 Well we found out that giving workers more up-to-date machines made them feel happier about the job and made them more willing to work harder.

   _____

   2 The steps we took to make people work alone meant that they found their work more worthwhile.

   _____

   3 It also meant they worked harder and got on better with their line managers.

B | Key notions: thoughts and ideas

1 **Match words 1–6 to definitions a–f.**

   1 a premise ___
   2 a theory ___
   3 a hypothesis ___
   4 a concept ___
   5 a model ___
   6 an approach ___

   a a description of a system or of how something works
   b a way of dealing with something/solving a problem
   c a formal set of ideas that is intended to explain why something happens or exists
   d a statement or idea that forms the basis for a line of argument
   e an idea or explanation based on a few facts that has not yet been proved true or correct
   f an idea or principle connected with something abstract

2 **Choose the correct option.**

   1 Their first attempt to find the cause failed so they tried an entirely new *premise/approach*.
   2 In my view, their *hypothesis/premise* won't stand up to close examination.
   3 Taylor formalized an entirely new *theory/concept* to explain how complex tasks could be broken down into a number of simpler ones.
   4 His entire theory is based on a false *approach/premise*.
   5 Maslow's *theory/concept* put shelter and safety as fundamental needs.
   6 Psychologists have suggested different *models/approaches* that explain the underlying elements of motivation.

3 **Complete the sentences with a word based around *hypothesis*.**

   1 I'd hardly call it a hypo_____; it's more a simple notion!
   2 There is no point trying to hypo_____, we need more facts.
   3 At the moment it is a purely hypo_____ situation.
   4 Well, hypo_____ speaking, it should be ready next week.
   5 They have put forward several hypo_____, all of them false.

Writing skills

| Paraphrasing other people's ideas

Paraphrasing, i.e. rewriting text in your own words, is an essential skill in academic writing. Paraphrasing can protect us against charges of plagiarism, which means directly copying other people's work and passing it off as our own.

1 **Study the list. Tick the suggestions that provide good advice for creating a paraphrase. Cross out those that you think are wrong and change them into good advice.**

  1 Add your own ideas. ___

  2 Keep to the original ideas of the source. ___

  3 Use synonyms and other forms of vocabulary replacement. ___

  4 Copy parts of the text word for word. ___

  5 Introduce your own opinion. ___

  6 Vary the grammar structures. ___

  7 Keep the same vocabulary as the original source. ___

  8 Acknowledge the original source. ___

2 **Which expressions refer to an opinion from a single source and which express a widely-held view from multiple sources?**

  a Her view is that …

  b It would seem/appear that …

  c Mayo suggested that …

  d It has been suggested that …

  e According to Taylor …

  f Many experts believe that …

  g Maslow is of the opinion that …

  h It is argued by some experts that …

  i A widely-held opinion is that …

  j Ouichi argues/contends/maintains/points out/ suggests …

  k In Skinner's opinion …

Single source: _____

Multiple sources: _____

3 **Read the paragraph and underline the different ways the writer uses to paraphrase different experts.**

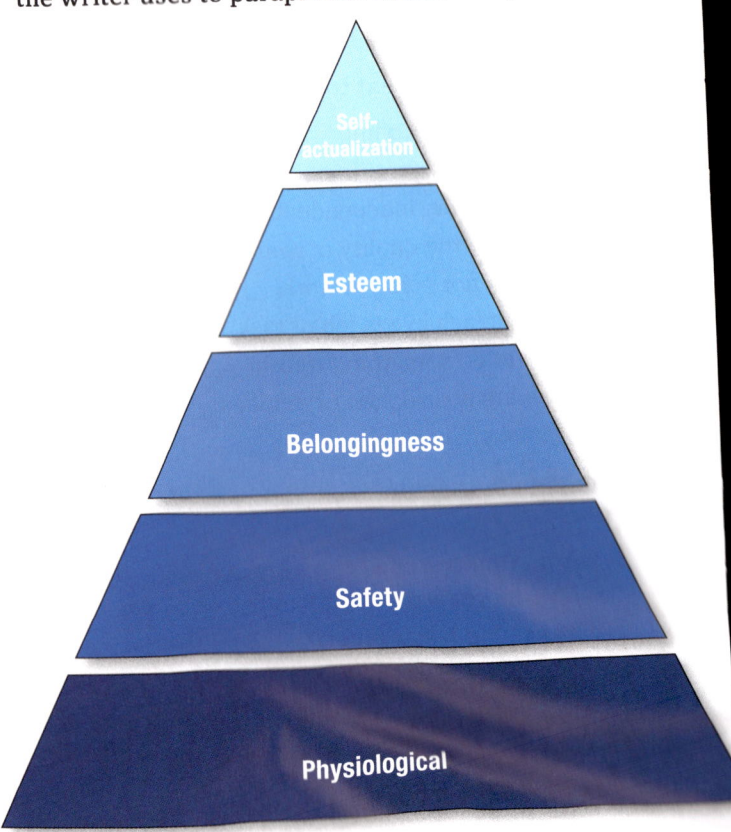

Most of us are familiar with Abraham Maslow's hierarchy of needs and its diagrammatic representation by a pyramid. In essence, the theory argues that only once basic physical and survival needs have been met can a person then go on to search for love, esteem and self-realization, found at the pinnacle of the pyramid. Although it is an intuitively satisfying theory it has come in for a certain amount of criticism from various researchers and thinkers. For instance, neither Wahba nor Bridewell have found concrete evidence to support this proposition, while Manfred Max-Neef argues that basic human needs are non-hierarchical and cannot be neatly separated out as Maslow suggests. Furthermore, Geert Hofstede, the Dutch social psychologist and anthropologist, criticizes Maslow's theory as being ethnocentric, focusing as it does on needs as perceived in an individualistic society, rather than reflecting the needs and values of collectivist societies. However, despite these misgivings, most of those working in the field of motivation acknowledge Maslow's contribution and would agree that his theory provides a useful point of departure for further research.

4 Study the following paraphrase of paragraph A on page 27. Match the sentences to the relevant part of the text.

a Nevertheless, research indicates that unforeseen negative results may ensue from the application of the methods of scientific management to predictable and uniform chores.

b What made it unique was the attention it paid to job design.

c Frederick W Taylor's pioneering work on job design known as 'scientific management' appeared in the early years of the last century.

d Taylor homed in on breaking operations down into closely monitored simplified tasks with a view to improving efficiency and performance.

e Elements that cast a shadow over its benefits include an increase in delays, a drop in motivation and output and the malicious destruction of job-related machinery.

5 What changes in the paragraph has the writer made to … ?

– Word order
– The order of ideas
– Grammar
– The choice of vocabulary

6 Write three paragraphs paraphrasing the opinions of the following theorists.

1 *McClelland – Theory of needs*

Three different types of motivating needs according to personality:

(i) need for power – want influence and control, like to be centre of attention.

(ii) need for affiliation – social recognition and affiliation important.

(iii) need for achievement – for people who like challenges and are afraid of failure.

2 *Vroom – Expectancy theory*

People will act in a certain way according to the attractiveness of the outcome that follows. The more attractive the outcome the better they will perform. The theory focuses on the relationship between performance and reward and the achievement of personal targets.

3 *J.Stacey Adams – Equity theory*

Motivation depends on how people think they are rewarded compared with others. Their input (work and effort) and outcome (rewards) need to be balanced and compare favourably with the inputs and rewards received by other people. An imbalance and feeling of unfairness will demotivate people. They will reduce the amount they work or may leave the organization.

Research task

1 Discover what you can about Douglas McGregor's theory of motivation known as Theory X and Theory Y. How does this theory fit into the overall framework of motivation theory? How does it correspond to Maslow's earlier work?

2 Find out how Ouichi has extended and expanded McGregor's work.

3 Find out what are the essential differences between the following theories.

McClelland's *Theory of needs*

Vroom's *Expectancy theory*

J. Stacey Adams' *Equity theory*

6 Culture

Study focus

1 What does it mean literally when a company goes international? What are the implications?

2 Think of three companies from your country that have gone international. Where have they expanded?

Reading strategies

A | Brainstorming ideas

1 You are going to read an extract from an article called *'Strategy and the multinational enterprise'*.

Define the terms

– strategy   – multinational enterprise

2 The extract examines the reasons why companies go international. Brainstorm your own reasons and make a list.

B | Scanning for specific information

Scan the text and match sentences 1–6 to the names of the academic experts a–f.

Who … ?

1 has provided a full list of reasons for going international ___

2 noticed that firms threatened by foreign competition at home, expanded abroad to survive ___

3 says that expanding abroad allows firms to acquire local know-how ___

4 claim that firms with widespread international operations perform better than those without ___

5 going international is a good way of exploiting unused resources ___

6 shows that going international helps firms that are dealing with tough domestic competition ___

a Mascarenhas
b Root
c Penrose
d Morck and Yeung
e Mitchell, Shaver and Yeung
f Tallman, Fladmoe-Lindquist

C | Reading for detailed understanding

1 Read paragraphs A to C and answer the questions.

1 What is the most commonly cited reason for the expansion of firms overseas?

2 According to traditional models, what happens to domestic markets as local firms become successful?

3 Why doesn't overseas expansion necessarily involve a corresponding increase in resources?

4 Why is the writer dissatisfied with the 'theoretical sequence' he has just outlined?

5 What benefits does being bigger bring to a business?

6 What advantage do firms with a greater geographical spread have over their less adventurous rivals?

7 What motivated the following companies to expand/ invest overseas?

a Sony and Honda in the US.
b Ford, BMW and Mercedes in 'Motorsport Valley'.
c Motorola in France.

8 What are the advantages of joint ventures overseas in R&D (research and development)?

2 Read paragraph D and answer the questions.

1 According to the author, how has the thinking about the protection of FSRCs evolved? (FSRC = firm specific resources and capabilities)

2 List the advantages and disadvantages of protecting FSRCs.

3 Why does the author believe that the best way of protecting FSRCs is to disseminate them as widely as possible through its products and partnerships?

D | Critical evaluation

Discuss these questions.

• How convinced are you by the Microsoft example that suggests that it benefits MNCs to share their know-how with suppliers?

• What say should governments have in the transmission of know-how to different countries? Are they ever justified in trying to prevent it?

Strategy and the multinational enterprise

A There are a number of traditional perspectives on why companies might go international. Many authors have listed many reasons, a particularly comprehensive list being provided by Root (1987). A common top consideration for most businesses as they expand geographically, whether locally, nationally, or internationally, is the desire to access larger markets. Even large domestic markets will be saturated by the successful firm as it expands distribution, increases its product range, develops new manufacturing sites, and so forth. Such a company, however, is likely to possess some resources that are not completely engaged, particularly managerial resources that increase with application and learning so that they can organize even larger operations efficiently. Penrose (1959) tells us that they are a response of the business firm to excess resources that are 'lumpy' or indivisible, so that they cannot be trimmed to fit its current position. The way to use up these resources is by continual expansion. Once the national market is filled, the business firm will turn to international markets. Of course, this is an extreme and theoretical sequence. The reality of many companies is that they turn rapidly to international markets, even as they expand domestically. The outcome and objective are the same, though, whether a company wants to fill every accessible corner of its national market or is looking to international possibilities early in its history. Larger operations open the way for economies of scale, faster access to learning curve effects, market power as buyer and supplier, and other benefits of size. As technology has improved, the efficient scale of more and more industries has become larger than any one market, even those of the largest industrial nations, can absorb. Therefore, increasing geographical spread allows firms to become more efficient and thus more competitive, while at the same time providing them with the market power to dominate smaller, weaker, less widespread competitors. And, indeed, Morck and Yeung (1991) – among many others – show that firms with extensive international operations often achieve superior performance.

B The benefits of size are commonly cited as important to multinational firms, but access to wide-ranging markets also improves the efficiency of smaller, smarter firms. The 'new economy' gives many examples of information age firms that seek regional and global audiences for their highly volatile products. Even in the old economy we see examples of such strategies. Mascarenhas (1986) showed in a study of second tier firms that such enterprises moved into international markets when they perceived that they could not overcome more powerful rivals in the home market. Well-known companies such as Honda and Sony, for instance, became fixtures in the American market while they were still struggling with Toyota and Matsuhita, respectively, in Japan. Also, Mitchell, Shaver, and Yeung (1993) found that firms facing foreign challenges in their home markets needed to expand internationally in order to survive. Wiersema and Bowen (2008) show that firms facing increasing industry globalization and foreign-based competition will demonstrate increased international diversification.

C However, international scope benefits multinational firms through more than just access to larger markets in which to exploit existing firm-specific resources and capabilities. Firms can also build new FSRCs through internationalization (Tallman and Fladmoe-Lindquist 2002), by tapping into areas of expertise in foreign countries or industrial clusters within those countries. Ford, BMW, and Mercedes all have held investments in small assemblers of racing engines within the so-called 'Motorsport Valley' of south-eastern England as a way to access cutting edge engine developments. Motorola Semiconductor developed its smartcard technology through acquisitions in France's high technology region around Grenoble and by maintaining the headquarters and product development for this product in France, where the technology was more advanced than at home in the US. R&D joint ventures in foreign countries can both adapt corporate technology to the local market and access local technology for application in wider markets by the MNE. Appreciation of the importance of 'sticky' local knowledge that can be

tapped by subsidiaries, but not relocated without
85 damage has increased greatly among both scholars and
practitioners in recent years (Markusen 1999).

D Protection of FSRCs, or their benefits, can also be
enhanced by internationalization. Older models of
the MNE focus on the risks of loss of competitive
90 advantage when FSRCs are exposed in foreign markets
and to foreign partners. These local risks do exist,
but can be managed. On the other hand, widespread
application of FSRCs reduces the possibility that their
benefits will be put at risk by application in only a
95 limited range of markets. If Microsoft did not offer
Windows, Office and its other products around the
world, local firms would develop competing products,
some of which could well become major competitors
even back in Microsoft's home North American market.
100 Local risks of intellectual property theft – a widespread
problem for Microsoft in some markets such as China –
are still less than the risk of not diversifying its markets
to protect income streams, compete with local firms
and other MNEs, and identify innovative applications
105 coming from unique contexts. Internationalization
presents some risk to competitive advantage, but

hiding behind regulatory, cultural, and market power
barriers in the home country out of fear of loss of
competitiveness backfires regularly – stagnation
110 of technological innovation kills more firms than
opportunistic partners and customers.

....

Source: Chapter 12 'Strategy and the multinational
enterprise' *Oxford Handbook of International Business,*
Oxford University Press, 2010

Glossary

cluster (line 69): a group of the same or similar businesses
gathered together in the same area/region

economies of scale (line 29): the fact that as the amount
of goods produced increases, the cost decreases

lumpy (line 17): a mass that is lumpy cannot easily be
separated into separate elements

saturate (line 08): to provide so much of a product in a
particular market that few new customers can be
found

subsidiary (line 84): a company owned or controlled by
another company

Business vocabulary

A | Organizational strategy

1 Match the words to form collocations from the text.

1	learning	**a**	advantage
2	cutting	**b**	property
3	income	**c**	stream
4	competitive	**d**	venture
5	intellectual	**e**	curve
6	joint	**f**	edge

2 Match the collocations from 1 to the definitions.

1 _____: the newest most
advanced stage of something

2 _____: regular payments; the
money a business receives

3 _____: something that helps a
company be more successful than its rivals

4 _____: a new company that is
started by two or more companies together

5 _____: an idea, design, etc. that
belongs to a person or organization that cannot be
sold or copied without the owner's permission

6 _____: the rate at which you
acquire a new subject or skill; the process of learning
from the mistakes you make

3 Complete the sentences using the collocations from 1.

1 You expect other people to respect our
_____, but it's OK for you to
illegally download movies!

2 The best way of entering some markets is through a
_____ with a local partner.

3 They claim that their technology is
_____, but I saw something
equally advanced at last month's trade fair.

4 The loss of that regular contract has badly affected
our _____ and led to cash flow
problems.

5 We are on a very steep _____
with this new software; we won't be fully operational
for another few weeks.

6 Singapore is an example of a country that created a
_____ by developing a highly
educated and skilled workforce.

**4 Choose collocations from 1 to comment on the
following.**

1 Describe an advanced product that is at the head of
what is currently available.

2 Talk about a time when you found it hard to learn a
new skill.

3 Predict the future of the software, publishing and
music industries in the light of the increase in people
illegally downloading material.

B | Collocations with 'market'

1 Search the text on page 33 for words that collocate with the word 'market'.

_____   _____
_____   _____
_____   _____
_____   _____
_____ **MARKET** _____
_____   _____
_____   _____
_____   _____
_____   _____

2 Add other words to the diagram to create further collocations. Example: *buyer's MARKET; MARKET leader.*

3 Create your own definitions for these collocations. Example: *a buyer's market is where the buyer has power over the seller in terms of the price he is prepared to pay.*

C | Organizational strategy word-building

1 Complete the sentences by changing the <u>underlined</u> word into a suitable form.

Example:

Finding new markets is our top consideration <u>consider</u>.

1 The _____ <u>acquire</u> of plantations in Brazil guaranteed their raw rubber supplies.

2 I am not sure how suited he is to a _____ <u>manager</u> role; his people skills aren't developed enough.

3 At the moment the concept is purely _____ <u>theory</u>; we'll have to see if we can make it work in practice.

4 _____ <u>diversify</u> isn't always the answer – sometimes it's best to stick with what you do best.

5 _____ <u>Geography</u>, they have a presence in 23 countries.

6 I think R&D have come up with a truly _____ <u>innovate</u> development.

7 The _____ <u>international</u> of our business has created some great career openings.

8 The purchase of the plant was an _____ <u>opportunity</u> move that won them lots of enemies.

9 3D TV will shortly become _____ <u>access</u> to average families.

10 Some commentators believe that _____ <u>global</u> has widened the gap between the rich and the poor.

2 Which of the answers from 1 are nouns, adjectives and adverbs?

3 What, if any, is the change in word stress between the word you were given and your answers?

Example:

consider   *consideration*
oOo   oooOO

Writing skills

A | Question analysis

Essay question analysis will help you to understand exactly what a question expects of you. Even small changes to a question can significantly change the expectations of the question. Key question words are important to understand as they indicate how you should approach the question. Brainstorming is a method used to generate ideas. These ideas can then be used to outline an essay and focus your further research and reading.

1 Look at the essay question and answer the questions that follow.

Briefly outline the major benefits of free trade before considering whether there is ever any justification for protectionism.

a What are the main topics of this essay question?

b Which part of the question asks for a description and which part asks for an evaluation?

2 Match words 1–6 to definitions a–f.

1 illustrate ___
2 compare ___
3 discuss ___
4 justify ___
5 outline ___
6 analyse ___

a to examine or judge two or more things in order to show how they are similar to or different from each other
b to talk or write about something in detail and consider different ideas and opinions about it
c to look at something carefully and thoroughly
d to say what someone or something is like by giving details or examples
e to give a good and acceptable reason for something
f to give brief main details

3 Two other features of an essay question are *focus and limitations*. Look at the essay question and answer the questions that follow.

Briefly outline the major benefits to China of free trade in the 21st century before considering whether there is ever any justification for protectionism.

a How is the focus of this question different from the one in 1?

b What limitation has been put on this focus?

B | Planning and organizing an essay

1 Study the essay question. With a partner write down all your ideas on this topic.

Briefly outline the major benefits of free trade before considering whether there is ever any justification for protectionism.

2 Compare your ideas to the ones below.

- Consumers can get a better price.
- Greater choice for consumers.
- Countries and companies can earn more money.
- Trade is less expensive.
- There is less bureaucracy.
- Trader is quicker and more efficient.
- Protectionism allows for countries to protect their own companies.
- Protectionist countries can still export.
- Companies that sell only in their own country do not have to worry about foreign competition.
- Salaries could be more protected.
- Job security could be higher.

3 Organize your ideas into the structure of an essay. Make sure there is a clear focus and topic for each paragraph.

4 Compare your draft plan with a partner. Make comments on:

- The order they have placed the ideas in.
- The focus chosen for each paragraph.
- Ideas they can expand on.
- Ideas that are missing.

5 Write your essay.

Research task

Sweden's *H&M*, and Spain's *Zara* are two fashion chains that have both expanded successfully internationally. Find out the evolution of the two businesses and what their similarities and differences are.

BENEFITS OF FREE TRADE

JUSTIFICATION FOR PROTECTIONISM

7 Organizational learning

Study focus

1 People commonly talk about 'learning organizations'. How is it possible for an organization to learn?

2 How is organizational learning different from how individuals learn?

Reading strategies

A | Understanding the relationship between text and graphic

1 Read paragraphs A and B of the text and label the diagram with the stages of Dixon's organizational learning cycle.

2 Read paragraphs A and B again. Dixon's model depends on clear information flow. How can the following contribute to this?

1 R&D
2 Job design
3 Information sharing
4 Relationships between members of different departments and levels of responsibility.

B | Reading for general understanding

Read paragraphs C and D. Which sentence best summarizes what they are about?

a How Ford rescued Mazda.
b Why Ford Europe has had to change.
c Japanese management's secrets of success.

C | Reading for detailed understanding

Answer the questions about each paragraph.

Paragraph C

1 What is an essential ingredient for a learning organization?
2 How was Ford Europe organized? How did this work against the overall good of the company?
3 What impact did Ford's organization have on ... ?
   a communication within the company
   b relationships between employees
4 What forced Ford to re-think how it did things?

Paragraph D

1 What two major problems faced Ford?
2 What key difference existed between the way Japanese car manufacturers organized themselves and Ford?
3 How was Ford able to tap into Mazda's expertise and way of doing things?
4 What four pillars does Mazda's simultaneous engineering rest on?
5 What lessons has Ford learned about ... ?
   a careers and job design
   b product design and production

D | Summarizing

Continue the sentences to produce a short summary about the problems facing Ford and the steps that it took to resolve them.

Towards the end of the 1980s Ford Europe was facing trouble because

_____

The problems emanated from

_____

The company's management realized

_____

Luckily for Ford it had

_____

From Mazda it learned that

_____

Accordingly, the company introduced the following changes

_____

E | Critical evaluation

Discuss these questions.

• It is generally accept that Japanese society is collectivist, while Western society is individualistic. How realistic is it for transcultural firms to expect its employees to adopt diametrically opposed mindsets?

• For several decades, Japanese companies have served as an example for others to follow. How far is this the case nowadays? Where should today's failing companies look for models to copy?

Organizational learning

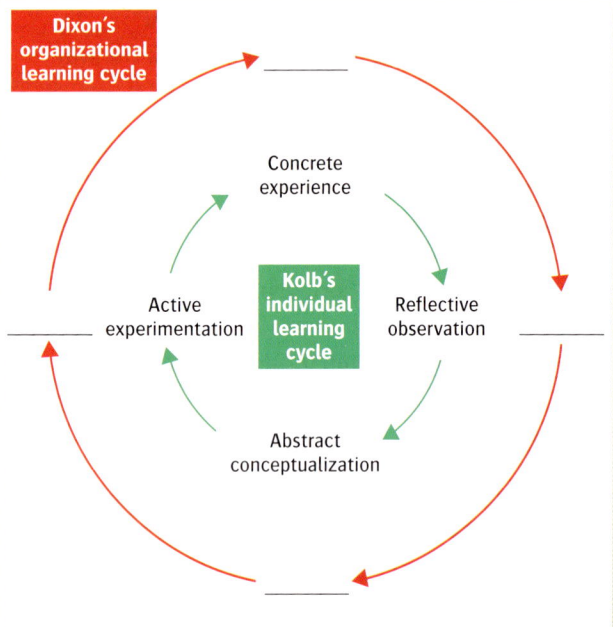

Dixon's organizational learning cycle

Kolb's individual learning cycle

Concrete experience

Reflective observation

Abstract conceptualization

Active experimentation

A The learning organization is about individual and organizational change and about creating the conditions for better learning. Dixon proposes that there is an 'organizational learning cycle', a way that
5 we can learn collectively. Dixon's cycle borrows heavily from work by Kolb, who is best known for his theory of individual, experiential learning. Dixon and Kolb's learning cycles are both four-stage processes of continuously revising and
10 creating knowledge. Kolb's experiential learning cycle proposes that an individual's learning progresses through four stages: concrete experience, reflective observation, abstract conceptualization, and active experimentation. The first stage requires generating
15 ideas through experience. During the second stage the individual integrates and reflects on the experience. The third stage involves drawing conclusions and abstracting lessons or concepts from the material experienced and reflected upon. The fourth stage
20 involves testing out theories or ideas, which returns the individual to seeking more concrete experience and so on.

B Dixon's organizational learning cycle is geared to the collective organization and not individuals. In
25 Dixon's organizational learning cycle, information is widely generated by utilizing the external and internal environments. It is collected continually and from multiple sources. Internally, it is generated by experimentation, analysis of mistakes and successes,
30 and the use of data for self-correction. Further, research and development is not the exclusive reserve of an isolated R&D department, but is conducted by

line management. Information is integrated into the organizational context by disseminating it accurately
35 and in a timely manner. The flow of information is unimpeded and employees are rewarded for accurate reporting on what they have found rather than just for saying what they think they are expected to say. Information sharing is encouraged through job design
40 that focuses on multi-skilling and multi-functioning. Where possible, staff positions such as personnel and marketing are integrated with line management. Information is collectively interpreted by encouraging all employees to discuss their different interpretations
45 with each other. Rather than funnelling information to a conclusion, individuals are expected to be more open-minded, flexible and questioning of their own points of view. Frequent interactions, keeping the organization limited in size, and treating everyone
50 equally are other methods of collective interpretation. Action is taken giving authority and control to the local level of the organization. This is done according to centrally agreed, critical specifications. There are no penalties for failure, when taking reasonable
55 risks, and the reward system uses profit sharing and stimulates committed and innovative action.

C The organizational learning cycle depends on a supportive organization structure and culture; further it assumes individuals will be motivated to learn.
60 Western companies have been criticized in the past for encouraging functionally divided careers that have motivated ambitious managers and employees to work for the good of their own work group and function rather than to the strategic benefit of the
65 company. Ford of Europe, a US company operating in Europe, had an organizational structure described as 'functional chimneys'. The functioning structure encouraged vertical communication and a high degree of specialization in areas such as finance, accounting
70 and product planning, but had the negative effect of making Ford employees internally competitive rather than focused as one group serving its automobile markets. Competition from overseas manufacturers, particularly Asian car manufacturers, became more
75 intense in the late 1970s and 1980s, forcing Ford executives to reconsider the effectiveness of both their business strategies and the internal organization. As is often the case for many companies across the world, it takes a big shock caused by a development in the
80 external environment to persuade managers of the need to act quickly and make fundamental changes.

D Starkey and McKinlay have researched Ford of Europe's improvement of the product development process. In short, Ford's costs were too high and the time-scale
85 too long. Japanese companies such as Mazda, Toyota and Honda were identified as leaders in product

development and their approach was very different from Ford's. These Japanese companies were more integrated and cross-functional organizations, using
90 distinct management practices. Ford learnt a lot from Mazda having a 25% equity stake in the company. It learnt from Mazda's successful practice of simultaneous engineering, judged to be a new approach and a step beyond matrix management (a popular form of
95 organization for innovation and project management in the engineering industry), because it operated with tighter coordination of product development and manufacturing. In 1989, Ford was facing the need to reduce its new product cycle time by eighteen months
100 just to become competitive. Ford had had problems in the past with either manufacturing dominating and compromising product design, or vice versa, product design remaining aloof from manufacturing leading to inefficiencies and operational problems. Both problems
105 were caused by compartmentalized thinking and a failure of functional integration. Mazda stresses four factors for simultaneous engineering: communication between product development and manufacturing; formal co-operation including cross-functional careers;
110 team culture and shared responsibility; and customer driven processes. Employee development in Ford will be of strategic benefit only where it can stimulate improved innovation and new ways of working. Following Mazda's example, an important part of the development process
115 is to facilitate increased lateral communication and decreased functional separation. Separate and isolated employee development programmes will not take the

company far enough in the highly competitive world automobile market. Employee development must occur
120 in improved cross-functional work environments and reinforce new structures of organizational learning. Managers and employees must learn to co-operate and integrate their activities more effectively rather than to co-exist under conditions of internal competition,
125 isolation and status divisions. The evidence then is that the structure and culture of Japanese corporations have been more successful than those of Western companies on sharing throughout the company, on-the-job-learning, teamwork and routine development of
130 subordinates by managers.

Source: Pinnington and Edwards *Introduction to Human Resource Management*, Oxford University Press, 2000

Glossary

abstract (line 13): based on ideas not on a real thing or person

to abstract (line 18): to draw the main points from a discussion

concrete (line 21): based on facts, physical things, not guesses

equity stake (line 91): having ownership in a company through holding shares

funnelling (line 45): to make something move/flow through a narrow space, as if through a funnel. We use a funnel to pour a liquid into say a bottle or tank

matrix (line 94): an arrangement of rows and columns

Business vocabulary

A | Learning processes

1 Find two-word expressions in the text to match the definitions.

1 learning through doing: e_____ l_____

2 first-hand knowledge: c_____ e_____

3 thinking about what you've seen: r_____
o_____

4 developing ideas: a_____ c_____

5 trying something out: a_____ e_____

6 deciding what you have learnt: d_____
c_____

2 Use the expressions from 1 to change this spoken text into a formal register.

'Well, I'm a great believer in learning through doing, and basing what I think on first-hand experience. Afterwards you can think about what you have done and seen, and make up your own mind.'

B | Departments in organizations

The text on page 38 mentions departments found in most organizations. Which one is responsible for … ?

a recording income and expenditure

_____

b handling capital

_____

c promotion and selling

_____

d staff development and recruitment

_____

e translating ideas into products

_____

f making things

_____

C | Verbs to describe experimental processes

1 Put sentences a–j in order to form a paragraph about a learning experience in a manufacturing plant. The first and last sentences have been done for you.

a We *determined* that a minuscule variation in one of the rings was the culprit. ___

b Furthermore, it *emerged* that the person responsible for quality control had been off sick. From interviewing staff we *inferred* that team spirit was poor. ___

c The experience told us that we needed to *instil* a desire for quality at each and every stage of the process. ___

d We *hypothesized* that a faulty component was responsible. ___

e It *transpired* that the job had been given to an inexperienced apprentice without supervision. ___

f It was decided to *test out* the theory by taking the motor to pieces and measuring each part. ___

g Finally, we *drew the conclusion* that teamwork needed to be improved. _10_

h We *deduced* that one of our machines had been wrongly calibrated. ___

i This incident forced us to *reflect on* what had happened. ___

j We needed to *ascertain* the cause of the problem as quickly as possible. _1_

2 Which of the words in *italics* in 1 mean … ?

a to become clear _____

b to establish _____

c to experiment _____

d to think about _____

e to decide _____

f to teach _____

g to learn _____

3 Describe a learning experience you have had in similar terms.

Writing skills

A | Opening and closing paragraphs

1 Put sentences a–e in a coherent order to form the opening/introductory paragraph of an answer to the below essay question.

Many businesses pride themselves on being 'learning organizations' To what extent do you think it is possible for organizations to learn?

  a Yet, business thinkers commonly refer to 'the learning organization' as though it were an animate organism able to gain knowledge through studying or reflecting on past experience. ___

  b In addition, this essay will discuss some of the implications of anthropomorphizing organizations and the impact that this can have on the people who work within them. ___

  c It will be argued that while organizations are strictly speaking incapable of learning, it is a useful term for describing knowledge management within progressive businesses. ___

  d An organization is not an animate being, therefore as such is incapable of independent thought and emotions. ___

  e This essay will discuss what we understand by the term 'the learning organization', and to what extent organizations can be said to learn. ___

2 Which sentence/s ... ?

  1 refers to a contradictory position

  2 states writer's starting position

  3 says what the essay will set out to show

  4 gives further information about the structure of the essay

3 Put sentences f–j in the correct order to form the closing/concluding paragraph.

  f This is, in the author's view, the true meaning of the term and the 'learning organization' which remains a useful metaphor, or piece of shorthand that we should not be afraid to use provided it is not taken or understood too literally. ___

  g Without this accumulated wisdom, each generation would be condemned to re-inventing the wheel. ___

  h Nevertheless, it has been argued that successful organizations have an important thing in common: their ability to preserve and transmit knowledge from one generation to the next which superficially corresponds to a teaching-learning relationship. ___

  i This essay has discussed what it means for an organization to learn, and considered some of the dangers associated with over anthropomorphizing their seemingly human behaviour. ___

  j So while organizations by their inanimate nature cannot 'learn', the term is taken to mean the context and systems that organizations provide that permit individuals to learn, refine and build upon the organization's accumulated wisdom. ___

4 How do the sentences that make up the closing paragraph correspond to the sentences in the opening paragraph?

B | Useful language

1 Match these lists of useful language for opening and closing paragraphs to the following categories.

  Stating what you have done
  Defining and narrowing
  Saying what you intend to do

  a _____

    For the purposes of this essay we shall focus ...

    We take the term X to mean …

  b _____

    In addition this essay will discuss ...

    This essay will examine ...

    It will be argued that …

  c _____

    This essay has examined ...

    This essay has argued ...

2 Study the essay question. Decide on your point of view and produce a thesis statement. Make a brief plan of the essay that you would write.

There is a widespread belief that, as well as training its people to fulfil a role, an organization has a wider responsibility for developing them more broadly as human beings. How far do you agree with this point of view? How realistic is this expectation?

3 Write the opening and closing paragraphs. As far as possible, use the concluding paragraph to refer to the issues raised in your introduction.

Research task

1 Find out about further theories of learning.

  • Behavioural learning theories including classic conditioning and stimulus generalization.

  • Cognitive learning theory.

2 How can these theories be applied to modern marketing?

8 Financing business

Study focus

1 Which economic sector do these activities belong to? How easy is it to decide where to put them?

   mining   retail   farming
   car-making   banking   shipbuilding
   education   hospitals   forestry
   textiles   steel-making insurance
   fishing

Primary	Manufacturing	Services

2 How does your country perform in these areas? Does it have a 'healthy' mix of activity, or does it rely too heavily on one sector?

3 Is your country's balance of trade, i.e. the difference between imports and exports, negative or positive?

Reading strategies

A | Using background knowledge to predict content

1 You are going to read a text about financial markets. What do you think is the role of the following markets?

1 The capital market

_____

2 The foreign (currency) exchange market

_____

3 The commodity market

_____

4 The insurance market

_____

5 The derivatives market

_____

2 Read the text and check your answers.

Type of market	Role
1	
2	
3	
4	
5	

B | Reading for detailed understanding

Answer the questions.

1 What are the key differences between direct investment and portfolio investment?

2 How did the derivatives market contribute to the financial crisis of 2008–2009?

3 How are financial markets different from markets in goods and services?

4 How does 'arbitrage' work?

5 What is the problem with the 'efficient market hypothesis'?

6 What is special about the US dollar, the yen, the euro and the British pound?

7 How stable was the euro – US dollar exchange rate between 1999 and 2004?

8 What impact did these rate changes have on trade between Europe and the US?

9 What was the underlying principle of the Bretton Woods system, and how effective was it?

10 What is the prevailing exchange rate system nowadays, how does it cope when countries display a trade deficit?

C | Critical evaluation

Discuss these questions.

• How was the financial crisis of 2007–2009 and directly afterwards handled in your country? Who suffered most?

• Is it right that traders in the financial markets can earn such high salaries and bonuses, while avoiding the consequences of their actions when things go wrong?

• Should countries be allowed to fix the value of their own currencies, or should they be obliged to 'float' or find their own value?

International financial markets

A International financial flows are necessary to facilitate trade, Foreign Direct Investment (FDI), portfolio investment, and lending by banks, governments and international financial institutions. The major
5 international financial markets include the capital market, foreign exchange market, commodity markets, insurance market, and derivatives markets. Multinational companies finance their international operations through share issues on the world's major
10 stock markets, by borrowing from a bank, or by selling bonds via a bank or securities trader (the 'over the counter' market) or sometimes on a stock market. The foreign exchange market enables currencies to be exchanged; currency exchange occurs in every
15 international transaction, either immediately or at an agreed future date, whether it involves trade in goods or services, investment borrowing and lending, insurance or any other financial transaction. The foreign exchange market therefore plays a particularly
20 important role in international business.

B Commodity markets involve the buying and selling of metals, oil, coffee, wheat, and other primary products; these products serve as raw materials, energy or unprocessed food supplies that are needed for the
25 production of goods and services and ultimately to meet the demand from consumers. International insurance markets enable companies to cover many of the risks of international business, either through individual insurance companies or through insurance
30 syndicates such as Lloyds of London which insures a large proportion of the world's shipping, airlines and other specialist activities or events. Finally, derivative markets create opportunities for trading in a wide range of financial products that are 'derived' from an
35 underlying asset such as a share, bond, commodity or currency, for example, at a fixed price on an agreed future date, allowing a firm to hedge against the risk of price fluctuations.

C Many of the funds used to buy shares, bonds,
40 commodities, and currencies are provided by portfolio investors, including individuals, companies, and financial institutions. Unlike direct investment, portfolio investment is concerned with the acquisition of financial assets or commodities for the purpose of earning a
45 return on surplus funds. Investors in these markets are interested in the financial return on an investment that does not involve control of a business operation. Many of these financial markets are highly specialized and involve transactions in the legal title to assets rather
50 than the direct handling of commodities, for example. They also facilitate the movement of vast funds around the world. Although these activities may appear to be peripheral to the movement of 'real' goods and services, or simply lining the pockets of successful portfolio

55 investors, the financial markets do in fact oil the wheels of the world economy. By making finance available, in the required form at the required time, the financial markets allow trade and investment to take place.

D Of course, financial markets do not always work as
60 efficiently as described above. This was certainly the case during the 2008–9 international financial crisis, following problems in the US sub-prime market which emerged in 2007. In this case, the complex derivatives markets had allowed high-risk assets to
65 be bundled into securities and sold on to investment companies and other financial institutions. Whilst this process appeared to spread the risk, it also meant that large amounts of assets held by a variety of financial institutions were at risk when sub-prime
70 mortgage holders started to default on their mortgage commitments. A number of banks had in fact expanded their lending to business and personal customers by borrowing heavily on the inter-bank market and the collapse in asset values caused the source of funds
75 to dry up, leaving the banks short of liquid assets to finance their day-to-day operations.

E Financial markets are often highly flexible markets, where prices respond immediately to fluctuations in supply and demand, unlike many markets for goods
80 and services, and they rapidly take account not only of current information but also of expectations about further events. This property of financial markets can be seen in the process of 'arbitrage', where funds are moved between markets whenever a higher return can
85 be earned, causing asset prices to equalize provided there is free movement of funds between markets. However, the view that financial markets always operate efficiently, known as the efficient market

hypothesis, has increasingly been challenged in recent
90 years. Financial markets certainly respond quickly
to a change in market conditions, but this does not
appear to prevent them from allowing a high-risk
situation to develop in the first place, especially when
unpredictable events precipitate a financial crisis. The
95 response of the international community to the 2008–9
financial crisis was to call for stronger national and
international regulatory frameworks to reduce the risk
of financial collapse in the future.

F **The impact of exchange rate movements**

One of the most influential factors affecting the
100 international flow of goods, service and investment
is the movement of exchange rates. Here we note the
significance of exchange rates for patterns of trade
and investment. Most of the world's major currencies,
including the US dollar, the euro, the Japanese yen
105 and the British pound are fully convertible floating
currencies. That is they can be traded anywhere
in the world and their value normally depends on
market forces.

H The euro/US dollar exchange rate since the launch of
110 the euro in January 1999 provides a vivid illustration
of the impact of exchange rate movements. On the 4th
January 1999, the first day of trading in the new euro,
the euro was worth $1.18. By October 2000 the euro
had slipped to 0.84 c, but by the end of December 2004
115 the euro had climbed back to $1.34. These movements
represent a depreciation in the value of the euro
of 28% between January 1999 and October 2000,
an appreciation of 58% between October 2000 and
December 2004 and a depreciation of 10% in the euro's
120 value during 2005. Such large fluctuation had a massive

impact on the terms of trade between Europe and the
USA during this period, that is, on the relative prices of
European and American goods and services.

H The prevailing view from 1945 to 1970 was that
125 exchange rates should be stabilized in order to provide
certainty in trading relationships. This period was
one of fixed exchange rates under the Bretton Woods
system, with the dollar as the anchor currency, and
the relative stability it brought probably helped to
130 encourage the steady growth in trade during the post-
war years. Exchange rate stability was one of the early
roles of the IMF, along with the provision of lending
facilities for countries with balance of payments
deficits. The Bretton Woods system of fixed exchange
135 rates was abandoned during the early 1970s and the
automatic adjustment mechanism of floating exchange
rates is now generally favoured. A floating rate finds
its own level and a country with a trade deficit will
find that its falling currency helps to boost exports and
140 restrain imports, thus helping to correct the deficit.

Source: Andrew Harrison *Business Environment in a Global
Context*, Oxford University Press, 2010

Glossary

bundle (line 65): a number of different things wrapped up
and sold together

facilitate (line 1): to allow/make something easier or
possible

legal title (line 49): proof of ownership

over the counter (line 11): as in a shop

underlying (line 35): important, but not easily visible or
obvious

Business vocabulary

| Financial vocabulary

1 **Find words in the text to match the definitions.**

1 _____: the practice of buying
something (for example shares or foreign money) in
one place and selling it immediately at a higher price
in another

2 _____: a thing of value that a
person or company owns

3 _____: an agreement by a
government or company to pay back the money an
investor has lent plus a fixed amount of interest on a
particular date

4 _____: a product or a raw
material, such as grain, cotton or metals that can be
bought and sold in large quantities

5 _____: the loss of value over a
period of time

6 _____: to fail to pay a debt

7 _____: a financial instrument
such as an 'option' or a 'future'

8 _____: to protect yourself
against the risk of losing money in the future because
of changes in the value of shares, currencies, raw
materials, etc.

9 _____: a loan from a bank to
buy a home

10 _____: a set of investments
owned by a person or organization

11 _____: a financial asset such as
a share or a bond

12 _____: the amount of a
company that a person owns, or a company's value
on an international exchange

2 Some words can have a number of different meanings. What non-financial meanings can you find for the following?

1 to share, a share

2 to stock, a stock

3 security

4 hedge

5 appreciate

6 bond

7 portfolio

3 Correct the financial vocabulary mistake in each sentence.

Example:

I don't like to invest all my money in the same thing, I like
          portfolio
to have a ~~bundle~~ of shares.

1 What you need to do is to protect yourself by fencing your risk.

2 Oil, grain and rubber are important assets which manufacturers around the world depend on.

3 My daughter-in-law does arbitration for a finance company, I don't quite understand what she does, but it is something to do with buying and selling shares.

4 The financial crisis was caused because so many borrowers defected on their loans.

5 I have got quite a lot of government shares; it's much safer because I don't think the country will ever go bankrupt.

6 I don't like to invest my money in deviations; they are too far removed from the original company.

7 I think he's a security guard for a bank in the city, but he drives a Mercedes and doesn't wear a uniform.

Writing skills

Incorporating sources

It is important to follow a number of conventions when using other people's ideas in your writing. It is also important to make sure the ideas you include flow naturally in your own writing.

1 Look at the following sentence from the text on page 43 and the two quotes a–b that follow it. List the differences you can see in these quotes.

Financial markets are often highly flexible markets, where prices respond immediately to fluctuations in supply and demand, unlike many markets for goods and services, and they rapidly take account not only of current information but also of expectations about further events.

a According to Henderson (2009:125) "Financial markets are often highly flexible markets, where prices respond immediately to fluctuations in supply and demand, unlike many markets for goods and services, and they rapidly take account not only of current information but also of expectations about further events."

b According to Henderson (2009) prices in financial markets changes quickly depending on supply and demand. They change much more rapidly than other markets and even change in response to beliefs about other events.

Differences:

2 Sentence a in 1 is a direct quote and sentence b is an indirect quote. Look at the definition of a direct quote and write a similar definition of an indirect quote.

A direct quote uses the exact words of the author of the original source. Using quotation marks shows that the exact words have been used. The information from the source required in the text is the page number, year and author.

An indirect quote …

3 **Look at the paragraph and identify features 1–4.**

The value of a currency can change rapidly and have a major impact on the costs of importing and export. As Henderson (1999) illustrates, the euro on its launch was worth $1.18 but just under two years later it was valued at 0.84c. Just over 4 years later it had risen to $1.34. Such changes will have a significant impact on a company's ability to export and also the cost of any imports. Such factors, that lie outside a company's control, make international markets very volatile to trade in.

1 Topic sentence
2 Verb used to introduce the quote
3 The indirect quote from another source
4 The comment on the other source

4 **Look at the two topic sentences a–b. Which topic sentence does the following quote best support?**

"A floating rate finds its own level and a country with a trade deficit will find that its falling currency helps to boost exports and restrain imports, thus helping to correct the deficit." (Henderson, 2009:125)

a Stable currency rates help to facilitate steady growth.
b A weak currency can provide benefits to certain companies.

5 **Look at how the author comments on Henderson's quote.**

According to Henderson (2009), prices in financial markets change quickly depending on supply and demand. This sensitivity unfortunately means that prices of shares and other such products are much more susceptible to the pitfalls of speculation that can lead to a boom and bust cycle.

Comment in the same way on the following quote.
"A floating rate finds its own level and a country with a trade deficit will find that its falling currency helps to boost exports and restrain imports, thus helping to correct the deficit." (Henderson, 2009:125)

_____

_____

_____

_____

6 **Use the following quote to develop a paragraph on the topic of 'The need for financial regulation'. Incorporate the features from 3 into your paragraph.**

"The response of the international community to the 2008–9 financial crisis was to call for stronger national and international regulatory frameworks to reduce the risk of financial collapse in the future." (Henderson, 2009:125)

_____

_____

_____

_____

_____

_____

_____

_____

_____

_____

_____

7 **Exchange your paragraph with a partner. Identify the features from 3.**

Research task

1 **Establishing the relative values of different currencies takes into account many different variables. The *Economist* magazine uses the single measure of the price of a McDonald's Big Mac! Find out how Burgernomics works.**

a What does it have to say about the currency of your country?

b How accurate and reliable do you think this is?

2 **Find out about the original use of hedging.**

a How is this different from the use of today's hedge funds?

b What is meant by having a 'long' or a 'short' position?

9 Product life cycles

Study focus

1 Business consultants and writers on business topics often use diagrams to explain models or their theories. What diagrams and models are you familiar with?

2 How useful do you think these are?

Reading strategies

A | Predicting content from a diagram

1 Look at the three diagrams in the text on page 48. What do you think the article will say about them? How are they different?

2 Read the text and check if your predictions were correct.

B | Reading for general understanding

Which description best fits the text?

The text examines and discusses …

a what happens when knowledge becomes over-generalized.

b the relative worth of different management tools.

c the drawbacks of the product trade cycle as a management tool.

d the fundamental contradictions at the heart of the product life cycle model.

C | Reading for detailed understanding

1 Look at what different businesspeople might say. Which <u>phase</u> of the product trade cycle are they describing?

a 'I guess it makes sense to produce them overseas – they can supply the local markets directly, besides labour costs are so much lower, aren't they?'

phase: _____

b 'It's strange to think that six years ago they were one of our main export markets. Now we are importing products from them that are virtually identical.'

phase: _____

c 'There are a whole lot of consumers within a fifty mile radius of the factory who are ready to pay a premium to get the product. My guess is that we'll sell out within a couple of weeks.'

phase: _____

2 Read paragraph D about *Sunsplash*. Are statements 1–8 True (T), False (F) or Not Given (NG)?

1 Product ideas flow from low-income countries to high-income countries.

T ___ F ___ NG ___

2 World bank loans enable low-income countries to construct their own facilities.

T ___ F ___ NG ___

3 Low-income countries inevitably respond by producing the product they had originally imported.

T ___ F ___ NG ___

4 Zimbabwe switched to a command economy.

T ___ F ___ NG ___

5 *Sunsplash* reacted to South African competition with its own export plan.

T ___ F ___ NG ___

6 *Susplash* lost over half its market share.

T ___ F ___ NG ___

7 *Sunsplash* tried to find an alternative to expensive machinery.

T ___ F ___ NG ___

8 Financial considerations prevented *Sunsplash* from modernizing.

T ___ F ___ NG ___

3 Read paragraphs E and F and answer the questions.

1 How can businesses make use of the concept of the product life cycle to decide the future of their products?

_____

2 How may a product's life cycle differ between markets?

_____

3 Why may it be difficult to apply the Boston Consulting Group's matrix to global markets?

_____

4 How can the BCG matrix help in the analysis of a firm's international market?

_____

5 Why do bricks appear immune to the product life cycle?

_____

The Product Trade Cycle

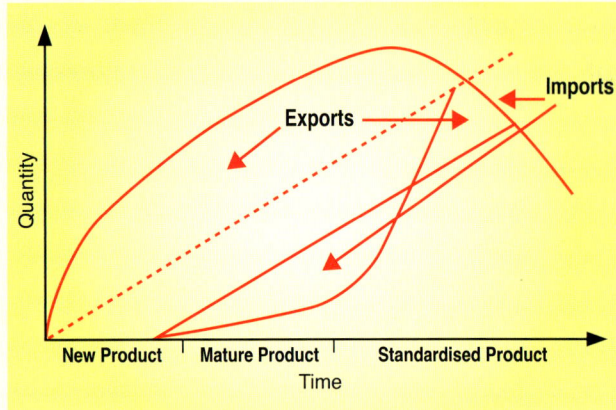

Figure 1: The product trade cycle

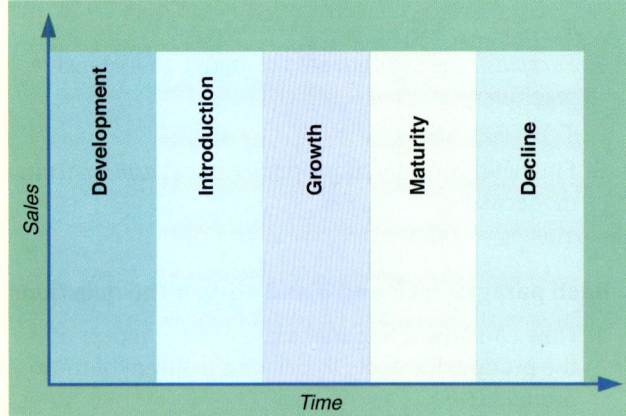

Figure 2: The product life cycle

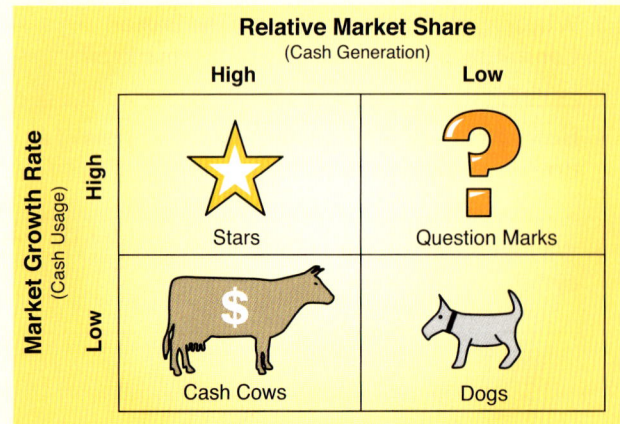

Figure 3: Boston matrix

A The product trade cycle or product life cycle (Vernon and Wells, 1968) suggests that many products go through a cycle during which high-income, mass-consumption countries which are initial exporters,
5 lose their markets and finally become importers of the product. At the same time, other countries, primarily developing countries move from being importers to exporters. These changes are reflected in Figure 1.

B An organization may decide to embark on an
10 international product strategy based on a number of factors:
– The company's overall market objectives
– Its decision on the resources to be committed to international development
15 – Market and customer expectations
– The products and services themselves
– Marketing mix support
– Environmental constraints
– Risk and control
20 The chosen strategy will be informed by international trade and product lifecycles. Other management tools such as the Boston Consulting Groups's growth share matrix will also inform the process.

The product trade cycle

C For a high-income country, phase 1 involves exporting
25 based on domestic product strength and surplus; phase 2 is when foreign production begins; phase 3 when production in the foreign company becomes competitive; phase 4 when import competition begins. The assumption is that new products are usually
30 launched in high-income markets because (a) there is greater potential, and (b) the product can be tested domestically near the source of production. Thus, new products usually emanate from high-income countries and when orders are solicited from lower-
35 income countries, so a thriving export market develops. Entrepreneurs realize that the markets to which they are selling have lower production costs, therefore production for the new products is relocated, so starts the second stage. Foreign and high-income country
40 production begins to supply the same export market. When foreign producers expand and gain experience, their competition displaces the high-income production source. At this point high-income-production countries begin to invest in foreign markets to protect their share.
45 As foreign producers expand, their economies of scale make them a source for third-country markets where they compete with high-income exporters. The final stages of the cycle occur when the foreign producer achieves such a scale that it starts exporting to the
50 original high-income producer at a production cost lower than its original high-income supplier. High-income producers then face competition at home. This cycle continues as the production capability extends

from other advanced countries to less developed
55 countries at home, then in international trade, and
finally in other advanced countries' home markets.

D The underlying principle behind the product trade cycle
is that it begins with export of new product ideas from
high-income countries to low-income countries and the
60 low-income countries begin production of the product.
Sometimes an exporter puts a product into a high/
low income country that is simply unable to respond.
The trade cycle then ceases to be the underpinning
concept. This may be due to a number of factors such
65 as lack of access to capital to build facilities, lack of
skills or that the cost of local production cannot get
down to the level of costs of the imported product. In
the latter case, product substitution may occur between
the exporter and importer. An example of the trade
70 cycle is that of *Sunsplash*. *Sunsplash* based in Mavingo in
Zimbabwe, produced a variety of fruit juices for the local
market. When Zimbabwe began its economic structural
adjustment programme in 1990, it moved from a
command (economy) to a market economy, part of which
75 allowed the free import of foreign products. The market
share of *Sunsplash* fell from 1 million litres annually
to 400,000 litres, primarily through imports from
neighbouring South Africa. On this reduced volume,
coupled with higher transport costs, the company could
80 not compete and closed down in January 1995. Other
problems included expenditure in imported machinery
which was hit by rising interest rates and the transition
to aseptic packaging which would have alleviated the
need for chemical preservations and enhanced un-
85 refrigerated shelf life. However, cash flow restraints
within the holding company (AFDIS) made the $5.8
million investment unviable.

E The product life cycle is also used as the theoretical
base for new or even existing product expansion. In
90 domestic marketing, the product life cycle has been
cited as a useful planning concept which could also
be used in international marketing. The traditional
five-stage life cycle – conception and pre-launch,
introduction, growth, maturity and decline, is well
95 documented. Attempts are usually made in the
maturity stage to extend the life cycle either by
introducing new products or extensions of existing
products. Extension may be made by introducing the
product into other markets. Not all markets are in the
100 same stage of the life cycle therefore what may be an
old product in one market, may be new in another. The
Boston Consulting Group's matrix of market growth
against market share is particularly complex when
applied to global markets. If competition is fierce,
105 relative market share by country and product may be
hard to assess, making it difficult to choose a retention,
growth or elimination strategy. Nevertheless, a matrix
analysis is useful in attempting to balance the portfolio
of international market involvement with the allocation
110 of investment funds. An analytical tool such as the
BCG matrix will also enable organizations to assess
the focus of their business.

F The product lifecycle and matrix approaches have
been subjected to critical review. Some products do
115 not go through the 'S' shaped product life cycle, for
example bricks, which show more of an undulating
cycle corresponding to surges and troughs in building
cycles. The matrix approaches have suffered from
the 'snapshot in time' syndrome and one of the major
120 problems is in predicting market growth rates and or
competitive share and investment accurately. When is
the right time to introduce a product to the market, or
delete one? Nevertheless, these concepts have survived
the criticisms and evolved to meet many of them, and
125 still remain often quoted and used as global strategy
conceptual building blocks.

....

Source: Chapter 8 of Kiefer Lee & Steve Carter *Global
Marketing Management*, Oxford University Press, 2009

Glossary

command vs market economy (line 74): In a command
    economy what is produced by whom, and in what
    quantities, to be sold at what price are all determined
    by central government. Ex-communist countries
    had command economies. In a market economy
    production and price are the result of the market and
    supply and demand and free competition
trough: (line 117): the lowest or bottom point
underpinning (line 63): providing essential support
underlying (line 57): something important but not
    immediately obvious or visible
undulating (line 116): moving up and down in a smooth
    wave-like motion

D | Critical evaluation

Discuss these questions.

- What is meant by the 'snapshot in time' criticism of the BCG matrix?
- What is the danger of saying that a product is nearing the end of its life
  cycle, or that it is a 'dog'?
- Are bricks products like any other, or are they more like a commodity?
  Can you think of other products that appear to defy the product life cycle?

Business vocabulary

A | Formal verbs

1 A feature of academic writing is the use of more formal vocabulary. Match the formal verbs from the text to their less formal definitions and synonyms.

alleviate	cease	emanate	embark	enhance
inform	occur	solicit	surge	thrive

ask for	stop	improve	come from
do lots of business/be successful	increase suddenly
relieve/make something less severe	happen
begin something new or difficult	influence/affect

2 'Translate' these informal spoken comments into a more formal written form using the verbs from 1.

1 Since we discovered the root of the problem, we have managed to reduce the damage.

_____

_____

_____

2 Before we begin a mass production programme we need to stop problems happening again.

_____

_____

_____

3 We don't need to stop making the old version, we just need to improve sales in new markets.

_____

_____

_____

4 If this sudden increase in interest rates carries on going, it will have an impact on our production costs.

_____

_____

_____

5 Since they asked us for our help their company has gone from strength to strength.

_____

_____

_____

B | Nominalization

1 Another feature of academic texts is the use of nominalization; that is using nouns instead of verbs or adjectives, for example. This has the effect of making a statement appear more formal. Search the text on page 48 for the noun forms we can make from the following words.

1 consume (paragraph A) _____

2 strong (paragraph C) _____

3 spend (paragraph D) _____

4 restrain (paragraph D) _____

5 retain (paragraph E) _____

6 grow (paragraph E) _____

7 criticize (paragraph F) _____

8 eliminate (paragraph E) _____

9 extend (paragraph E) _____

2 Look at the example and create further pairs of sentences with the words from 1.

'If we eliminate this product range a lot of people will criticize us'

= 'The elimination of this product range will result in a lot of criticism.'

C | Homographs

Some words look the same but have a different pronunciation and meaning. Look at the example and then read the other pairs of sentences aloud. How are the words different in meaning and pronunciation?

0a *It is an interesting <u>subject</u>.* /ˈsʌbdʒikt/ *(topic)*

0b *Why do you want to <u>subject</u> us to this?* /səbˈdʒekt/ *(make us endure)*

1a We are going to <u>object</u> to the new proposal.

1b What is the <u>object</u> of this exercise?

2a I would like to <u>present</u> our new strategy.

2b What would you say if I gave you a <u>present</u>?

3a The new government decided to <u>appropriate</u> all foreign held assets.

3b Make an <u>appropriate</u> suggestion.

4a We were <u>content</u> with the decision.

4b Have you studied the <u>content</u> of the contract?

5a The firm should move production <u>closer</u> to the domestic market.

5b She is a real <u>closer</u>, she's our best sales executive.

Writing skills

A | Problem solution essays

One common piece of academic writing is a problem solution essay. A key element of this is to evaluate the strengths and weaknesses of the possible solutions. When choosing a best solution it is important to be systematic in your approach. One method that can help is a paired comparison.

1 Look at the following problem. Work with a partner to think of as many different solutions as possible.

A company has high production costs.

2 Draw a grid like below on paper. You will need enough columns and rows for each of the solutions you thought of in 1.

	Solution A	Solution B	Solution C	Solution D
Solution A	✗			
Solution B	✗	✗		
Solution C	✗	✗	✗	
Solution D	✗	✗	✗	✗

3 Compare each solution against another. So for example in the blue box you are only comparing A against B. Write the solution that is best in each box.

B | Evaluative language

1 Look at the following sentences. Underline the word or phrase that indicates either a strength or weakness.

1 The Boston Matrix can be considered flawed in that it only provides an overview at any one moment.

2 Whilst an interesting theory the idea has never been tried before and thus lacks proof that it can be effective.

3 The solution only addresses the short-term concerns and is inadequate as a long-term plan.

4 Unfortunately there is insufficient data to make this theory transferable to other contexts.

5 The Boston matrix provides an effective tool for identifying the strategic strength of a company.

6 The solution clearly addresses the problem in the short-term.

7 This solution is likely to resolve a number of the underlying issues in society.

2 Use the words from 1 to replace the word or phrase in *italics* in the following sentences. More than one answer may be possible.

1 The policy was put in place to *deal with* the issue of long-term unemployment.

2 The solution is *weak* due to the practical implications of the plan.

3 Many politicians support the idea even though it *doesn't have enough evidence.*

4 The financial measures put in place are *unacceptable* for the scale of the problem.

5 The time available is *not enough* to implement such a plan.

6 It is surprising this solution has not been proposed before as it *evidently tackles* the key issues.

7 Of the options available this is perhaps the most *sound* in satisfying all parties concerned.

C | Writing practice

1 Look at the paragraph below. What is the function of each sentence?

a strength of the solution

b describing the solution

c weakness of the solution

d exemplifying the solution

[1]One possible solution for the company is to look for an outsourcing alternative. [2]For instance, a firm could be contracted to produce all or part of the product. [3]Whilst making such a move would clearly address the production costs the company is incurring there are also a number of concerns. [4]One particular flaw is that the product needs to be quickly delivered to market and the likely location of possible outsourcing firms means this might not be feasible.

2 Look at your solutions to the problems in section A again and write an evaluative paragraph for two of the solutions.

3 Look at a partner's paragraph. Try to identify the four features from 1.

Research task

Two more management tools are:

'The General Electric Grid' and 'The Ansoff product/ market matrix.'

1 Research one/both of them and explain the underlying principles that inform them.

2 Say how they work in practice.

3 Evaluate any criticisms or counter arguments.

10 Leadership

Study focus

1 Each year, people buy millions of books about leadership. Why are these books so popular?

2 How much can one learn about leadership or management from 'self-help' books? Can you name any of these books?

Reading strategies

A | Skimming for gist

Read the text. Which sentence best summarizes each paragraph?

Paragraph A
1 Leadership is a tangible skill.
2 Leadership exists only in people's minds.

Paragraph B
1 Researchers are sceptical about the ideas contained in popular books on leadership.
2 Researchers accept that popular books on leadership deal with some essential truths.

Paragraph C
1 Research indicates that followers are generally passive and willing to be led.
2 Heroic leadership appears to receive too much emphasis.

Paragraph D
1 Research appears to highlight the link between expectation and performance.
2 Despite a commonly held belief in the connection between expectation and performance, this has yet to be shown.

B | Scanning for specific information

Match the management experts to opinions 1–11 below.

Krohe   Murphy   Ruth   McNatt
Meindl & Ehrlich   Vroom and Jago
Carmeli and Shaubroeck   Padilla, Hogan and Kaiser
Bligh and Meindl   Bennis   Schriesheim

Who ... ?

1 maintains that leadership has no commonly held definition

2 thinks that the influence leaders have on organizations is exaggerated

3 reminds us that followers can sometimes oppose leaders

4 points out that leaders need to show they believe in themselves

5 says that some leadership books offer 'miracle cures'

6 claims that 'heroic leaders' receive too much focus

7 believes that books on leadership are essentially non-scientific

8 tells us that leadership books are full of sayings and easy answers

9 suggests that successful leadership depends on followers going along with what the leader and others decide

10 implies that the Pygmalion effect can work

11 describes the conditions that create for destructive leadership

Leaders and followers

A Leadership continues to dominate the focus of individuals seeking to understand and advance organizations, and thus the literature on leadership has attempted to provide a solution for seemingly endless
5 problems that confront organizations. Leadership is ultimately an abstract concept invented by people trying to understand their experiences and identity. While leaders, followers, and situations are indeed observable, leadership itself has no physical form and
10 is constructed in the minds of observers. Individuals who accept the subjective nature of leadership are less susceptible to "naïve realism" which leads them to assume that their perceptions are reality rather than a construction of goal-focused ideas. Further, despite
15 the popularity of leadership, the term is not a scientific term and has no formal or standardized definition (Vroom and Jago 2007).

B Bligh and Meindl's (2005) investigation of popular leadership books found that they were primarily
20 written outside the scientific or research-based approach to the field of leadership. The most common focus was the leader–follower interactions and most projected romantic views of leadership and its potential. They concluded that readers' appetite
25 for leadership books is satisfied in distinctive ways and these were to (a) fascinate the readers with the seemingly inexhaustible power and influence for leaders to enact change; (b) provide easy answers to the ever-quickening pace of change; (c) satisfy the
30 need for wisdom; (d) provide tools from individuals who claim expertise and vast experience; and (e) satisfy a capitalistic, consumer-driven society's desire for self-improvement. According to Krohe (2000, 19), "interest [in leadership books] is ignited by the promise
35 of a miracle cure" where the reader assumes they are already a leader and optimistically can achieve what these books market. The most commercially popular books satisfy the need for simple, understandable, and actionable answers to vexing problems (Schriesheim
40 2003) and are filled to the brim with maxims (e.g., trust your people). However, these maxims come without sufficient information about how the situational variables determine success or failure (Vroom and Jago 2007) and therefore these books may not transform
45 well-established and tested ideas into more effective organizational practices. Rousseau and McCarthy (2007) argue that managers should be educated from an evidence-based perspective that involves mastering valid behavioral principles and developed procedural
50 knowledge from practice, feedback, and reflection.

C Heroic leaders have always commanded a disproportionate amount of attention (Bennis 2007). This has led to followers and situations being largely ignored and has produced a predominately
55 romantic view of leaders generally. The tendency to create overly heroic and exaggerated views of leaders and their achievements, termed "romance of leadership", is enhanced by situations where causality is indeterminate and unpredictable events occur (see
60 Meindl, Ehrlich, and Dukerich 1985). Such adverse

situations, when combined with susceptible and needy followers, can enable destructive leaders to emerge (Padilla, Hogan, and Kaiser 2007). While the need for leaders to display confidence in their conviction and
65 to use a leadership style that conveys efficacy and control is widely recognized (Meindl, Ehrlich, and Dukerich 1985), Boerner, Eisenbeiss, and Griesser (2007) argue for greater focus on the desired outcomes rather than leadership style. In fact, Vroom and
70 Jago (2007) support disentangling the definition of leadership from organizational effectiveness because many factors, apart from the quality of leadership, have a significant impact.

"Many studies have simply assumed that leaders are
75 powerful and in control while followers are largely powerless, passive, and predictable. Little research attends to followers and their interaction with leaders" (Collinson 2005, 1423). Followers are romantically and unrealistically viewed as "simple" and impatient
80 for the right type of influence given by their leader. In fact, followers may actively attack and isolate leaders in order to reduce their ability to influence (Ruth 2006). While studies that treat followers in a more realistic and proactive light are evident (e.g., Boerner,
85 Eisenbeiss, and Griesser 2007; Densten and Gray 2001), leaders remain the focal point of leadership research and the most prominent element of the socially constructed realities about organizations (Meindl, Ehrlich, and Dukerich 1990) which has led
90 to an overestimation of the influence leaders have on organizational performance (Murphy 2002). Further, the idea that leaders and followers can easily rise above and overcome an inhibiting working environment (e.g., lack of resources) perpetrates romantic notions
95 of leadership; along with the notion that leadership is always associated with positive outcomes.

D Challenging performance expectations from leaders and followers can create pressure that motivates them to perform at a higher level. This unique
100 relationship goes beyond leaders and followers simply understanding the expectations of others better which then results in enhanced performance. Rather it acts like a self-fulfilling prophecy where expectation has a profound influence on the leader and follower. This
105 effect is called the [1]Pygmalion effect and operates subconsciously (see White and Locke 2000). According to McNatt (2000, 314), "the Pygmalion effect is a special case of [self-fulfilling prophecies] whereby a person's (perceiver's) expectations of another (target)
110 are transferred to, or otherwise have an influence on, the target such that the target ultimately modifies his or her behaviors or achievement level in conformity with the expectation." In other words, the raising of expectations of the leader or follower (i.e., the Galatea
115 effect) changes the belief that they can achieve, and thus their changed behaviors may result in higher performance. Leadership research appears to imply that successful leadership depends on followers' recognition and compliance with the expectations

120 of others, particularly their leader (Carmeli and Schaubroeck 2007). A dark side of the Pygmalion effect also exists (i.e. the [2]Golem effect) and represents the influence of negative expectations from a leader which subsequently reduces their follower performance. This
125 simplicity of the relationship between expectations and performance has been challenged (see McNatt 2000; White and Locke 2000). However, the basic idea that interpersonal expectations are a key influence in the self-beliefs which impact on performance is reasonably
130 robust. Further, this effect is most likely continuous and two-way, as both leaders and followers attempt to influence the other's self-belief of what is realistically achievable.

··

Source: Iain L. Densten *'Leadership: Current Assessment and Future Needs' in Oxford Handbook of Personnel Psychology,* Oxford University Press, 2008

Glossary

disproportionate (line 52): more than is appropriate/ deserved

filled to the brim (line 40): if a glass is filled to the brim there is no room for another drop

maxim (line 40): a phrase or expression that says what is usually considered to be true, or how people should behave

self-fulfilling prophecy (line 103): an event (usually negative) that is made to happen as a result of believing it will

vexing (line 39): difficult/worrying

[1] **Pygmalion and Galatea**
This story is an ancient Greek myth. Pygmalion is a sculptor who creates a statue of the perfect woman. He falls in love with his creation. The goddess Aphrodite takes pity on Pygmalion and turns the stone statue into a living woman, Galatea.

[2] **Golem**
From Jewish legend. A creature created by its master that carries out its deeds. The Golem has a dark and violent side.

C | Reading for detailed understanding

Answer the questions about each paragraph.

Paragraph A

1 What explains the high level of interest in leadership?
2 Where does leadership exist?
3 How does recognizing leadership as a subjective notion offer a form of protection?

Paragraph B

4 According to Bligh and Meindl, what is the main focus of self-help leadership books?
5 What is the drawback of an approach based on 'maxims'?

Paragraph C

6 What is the 'romance of leadership'?
7 What is the traditional view of the relationship between leaders and followers? Why may this be unrealistic?

Paragraph D

8 How does the Pygmalion effect work?
9 What is the Golem effect?
10 How does the author of the extract sum up the relationship between leaders and followers?

D | Critical evaluation

Discuss these questions.

- The writer seems critical of the notion of 'romantic, or heroic leadership'. However, are some leaders romantic and heroic?
- Have you ever seen the Pygmalion (or for that matter, the Golem) effect in action?
- The writer seems to criticize 'self-help' books for their lack of scientific rigour. Nevertheless, can we still learn useful lessons from them?

Business vocabulary

A | Adjectives to describe leaders and followers

1 Match adjectives 1–8 to definitions a–h.

1 conformist ___
2 naïve ___
3 compliant ___
4 proactive ___
5 romantic ___
6 passive ___
7 predictable ___
8 heroic ___

a lacking knowledge and good judgement, ready to believe what you are told
b having an attitude to life where imagination and emotions are especially important
c thinking and behaving in the same way as most other people
d behaving in an expected and often boring way
e showing extreme courage and determination
f too willing to agree with others and to follow rules
g controlling a situation by making things happen, rather than waiting for them to happen
h accepting what happens without trying to change anything

2 **Complete the sentences using the adjectives from 1.**

1 You need to be much more _____; people won't support you unless you show them who you really are.
2 Her defence of the company was really quite _____; nobody could have overcome the odds in the way she did.
3 He has a far too _____ view of life, he thinks that strong emotions count more than reason.
4 Looking back I wonder how I could have been so stupid and _____ to follow her the way I did.
5 He is far too _____; he'll do anything you tell him, whether it's right or wrong.
6 I wish you weren't so _____ all the time, you just wait for things to happen to you.
7 He is so _____, I could have told you he would react in that way.
8 It's not a crime to be different; you don't have to be so _____ all the while.

B | Word-building: negative prefixes

1 Negative prefixes such *dis-*, *in-*, *mis-*, *ir-*, *il-*, *un-* denote a negative sense to the rest of a word. Find examples of negative prefixes in the text on page 53.

_____

_____

_____

2 Complete the sentences using the word in brackets with a negative prefix. Make any other changes you think necessary.

1 Don't bother reading that article. Their methods are _____ (science) and _____ (logic).

2 His _____ (patient) and the _____ (predict) of his moods witnessed a rise in his _____ (popular).

3 Our _____ (tangle) from this research is essential, our reputation for _____ (reproach) must stay intact.

4 _____ (reason) expectations of leaders can lead to _____ (loyal) when unmet.

5 They seem to have an _____ (exhaust) supply of data; I wonder how they generated it.

6 People were persuaded by his arguments _____ (respect) of their age and background.

7 Their CEO is completely _____ (trust); he has been involved in a number of _____ (legal) transactions.

8 I'm afraid that these projected sales figures are both _____ (real) and _____ (achieve).

9 His reaction was _____ (mature) and _____ (proportion) to the harm he had suffered.

10 It was a terrible _____ (calculate) that led to the firm's _____ (do).

C | Synonyms

1 Using a variety of synonyms in your essay writing will make your texts more interesting as well as linguistically varied.

Put the words in the list into pairs or groups according to their meaning.

conviction	perspective	factor	result
viewpoint	robust	goal	belief
focus	idea	concept	perception
target	focal point	opinion	notion
element	outcome	strong	

2 We can use synonyms to avoid repetition. Match 1–5 to a–e. Make sure that your choice uses the appropriate synonym.

1 Leaders should never be afraid of a different viewpoint, … ___

2 Some firms have a strong belief in charismatic leadership, … ___

3 Managers should never worry if team members move the focal point of meetings to other matters, … ___

4 It's a great idea, … ___

5 Reserving praise for successful outcomes … ___

a such a conviction can be made to work in the leader's interests.

b can discourage staff from aspiring to riskier and less achievable goals.

c sometimes a new perspective can provide an important insight into the thinking of the team.

d sometimes shifting focus can reveal the team's concerns and anxieties.

e customers will go for such an exciting concept.

3 Use further pairs of synonyms to create sentences of your own.

Writing skills

A | Presenting opinions: introductory adverbs

Introductory adverbs can signal the writer's point of view. Replace the words in *italics* in 1–8 with adverbs from the list.

understandably	regrettably	accordingly
personally	hopefully	clearly
admittedly	consequently	

1 *It is a pity that* _____ most people are ready to believe what they read in self-help books.

2 *As a result* _____ they are often left with feelings of inadequacy.

3 *In my opinion* _____ I think that we should treat what we read with scepticism.

4 *I accept that* _____ some books may contain some useful advice for readers.

5 *I can appreciate that* _____ people are often faced with difficult situations at work.

6 *If all goes well* _____ people will think twice before following dubious advice.

7 *It seems obvious to me that* _____ no two situations are ever the same.

8 *Following on from this* _____ people believe that they can simply apply the advice to any vaguely similar circumstances.

B | Presenting opinions: modifying adverbs

Modifying adverbs can show the writer's opinion and degree of feeling. They appear before adjectives and verbs.

Example:

I was deeply disappointed with his latest book on leadership.

Complete the sentences by putting the words in the correct order and adding a modifying adverb from the box to strengthen the author's opinion. You can use an adverb more than once.

completely   totally   deeply   entirely
wholeheartedly   profusely

seek   is   books   understandable   it   people
advice   why   from

1 It is _____

_____

assume   to   unprepared   leadership   themselves
role   a

2 They may feel _____

_____

this   in   depressing   ideas   guide   the   contained

3 However, I found _____

_____

evidence   assertions   these   by   scientific   are
unsupported

4 Unfortunately, its _____

_____

appear   to   with   any   suggestion   agree
outrageous

5 Sadly, readers' reviews _____

_____

for   should   complete   printing   such   apologize
nonsense

6 Nevertheless, in my view, its publishers _____

_____

C | Approaching essays

1 Essay questions may ask us to give our opinion on a topic or discuss a proposition. We often set out our opinion in an opening paragraph. Look at the example essay question.

Some people would argue that leaders are born rather than made, while others maintain that leadership is a skill that can be learnt like any other. If we accept the latter to be true, how can people discover and develop their inner leader?

Read the introductory paragraph to an answer to the essay question and answer questions 1–2 below.

In recent years there has been growing interest in the topic of leadership. Countless books and DVDs feed the notion that everyone can be a leader. On-line programmes seduce us with promises that the keys to leadership success are a click and a credit card payment away. Quite understandably, ambitious executives operating in a cut-throat world are disposed to accept advice from any quarter. While I totally sympathize with people's aspirations to become leaders I am deeply depressed by the cynicism of the false-hope merchants and self-styled gurus who exploit this craving to line their pockets. Personally speaking, I believe that leadership is by and large innate. I shall argue that there is little one can do to maximize a skill that is not present within an individual in the first place. It is nature not nurture that counts. However, I do believe that where people have demonstrated leadership skills that these can be developed considerably. In the rest of this essay I shall investigate how leadership skills may best be cultivated.

1 What is the writer's point of view?

2 How does the writer's choice of vocabulary give his opinion away?

2 **Choose one of the essay questions below and write the opening opinion paragraph. Use modifying adverbs to strengthen your opinion.**

1 'Managers do things right, leaders do the right thing'. How far do you agree with this point of view?

Given that most leaders are drawn from the ranks of managers, how do leaders acquire the skills they need for their new role?

2 Some businesses send staff members on adventure programmes to encourage team building and/or develop leadership skills. What are the underlying principles that underpin such kinds of training? In your view, what are the benefits and drawbacks of such types of programme?

Research task

1 **Who were Sun Tzu and Niccolo Machiavelli? When did they live and what did they write?**

2 **Go to an on-line bookstore such as Amazon and search for management books that have been based on these two writers.**

3 **What claims are made about their usefulness in today's business world?**

4 **How true or universally valid are Sun Tzu and Machiavelli's thoughts to our day and age?**

Doing good by doing business

Study focus

Read the quotation and discuss the questions below.

'There is one and only one social responsibility of business: to use its resources and engage in activities designed to increase its profits so long as it stays within the rules of the game, which is to say, engages in open and free competition without deception or fraud.' (Milton Friedman US economist 1912–2006)

1 Is the sole purpose of a business to increase its profits?

2 Can a business have a broader, social purpose too?

3 Are social aims and profit aims compatible?

Reading strategies

A | Predicting content from an introduction

Read the introductory paragraph of the text and answer the questions.

1 What is one of the main criticisms of globalization? Why doesn't it apply to most of the world's poor?

_____

2 How do social entrepreneurs try to tackle the issue of poverty?

_____

3 What do you think the rest of the article will deal with?

_____

B | Identifying main ideas

Read the text. Match summary sentences 1–6 to paragraphs B–G (one paragraph does not have a summary sentence below).

This paragraph …

1 introduces someone with a thirst for social justice who never forgot his roots. ____

2 sets out the financial success of a modern co-operative. ____

3 explains how small interest-free loans can help to transform poor people's lives. ____

4 demonstrates how poor people with different jobs can band together to be stronger. ____

5 shows how exploiting new technology can forge links with new trading partners. ____

C | Reading for general information

Read the text again and complete the chart.

Organization/ Founder	Where it works	Its focus	Who it helps	How it helps
Grameen bank Founder: _____				
SEWA Founder: _____				
WESA Founder: _____				
TransFair Founder: _____				
APAEB Founder: _____				

D | Reading for detail and inference

Answer the questions.

1 What is the 'value-added chain'?

2 Why would the people the Grameen bank helps be unable to borrow money from a normal bank?

3 What social benefits does a loan from the Grameen bank bring?

4 What is unusual about SEWA?

5 How has up-to-date technology helped small businesswomen and coffee growers?

6 What impact has APAEB had in the broader economy of Bahia?

7 What do researchers hope to find out from a visit to APAEB?

8 How does the writer feel about Ismael Ferreira?

Social entrepreneurship

Introduction

A Much of the criticism of economic globalization has centered on factory labor abuses, but the majority of the world's poor are not employed in factories; they are self-employed – as peasant farmers, rural peddlers,
5 urban hawkers and small producers, usually involved in agriculture and small trade in the world's vast 'informal' economy ('informal' because economists have difficulty measuring it). Social entrepreneurs seeking to alleviate poverty among this target group
10 usually begin by asking: How can we help these producers benefit more from their trade and productive activities? And the solution they usually come up with is to change market conditions or re-design the 'value-added chain' for whole classes of small producers.

B Social entrepreneurs have attacked this challenge from many different angles. Some like Mohammad Yunus of the Grameen Bank, focus on access to capital. The Grameen Bank had pioneered and popularized a methodology for extending small, collateral-free loans
20 for self-employment to some of the world's poorest people. Founded in 1976 by Bangladeshi economics professor, Mohammad Yunus, by 2007 the bank had lent $6.1 billion to 7.1 Bangladeshi villagers, 97 per cent of them women. With the additional income that
25 Grameen's working capital loans bring, millions of villagers are better able to feed their families, build tin-roof houses (that keep them dry during the monsoons), send their children to school and accumulate assets for old-age security. With small amounts of working capital,
30 villagers can purchase assets, increase their productive capacity, and capture profits that historically have accrued to money lenders and land owners.

C Some focus on market relations. In Ahmedebad, India, the Self-Employed Women's Association
35 (SEWA) founded by Ela Bhatt, has helped 960,000 self-employed women, including paper pickers, cigarette rollers, kite makers, and vegetable vendors, organize themselves into a powerful trade union. SEWA not only protects its members from
40 exploitation and promotes government policies favourable to the informal sector, it also offers a range of services – collective purchasing, credit and savings, legal representation, health and child care, and insurance – that enable poor women to work
45 for themselves more profitably while reducing their exposure to business and personal risks.

D Some focus on market access. The Association pour le Soutien et l'appui de la Femme entrepreneur (Women Entrepreneurs Support Association),
50 founded by Gisèle Yitamben, in Douala, Cameroon, helps small businesswomen in West Africa – fruit growers, craftswomen, French-English translators – market their products and services to European buyers via the Internet. Similarly, TransFair, USA,
55 based in Oakland, California, founded by Paul Rice, links small coffee growers in Latin America to major US coffee retailers, such as Starbucks, Safeway and Green Mountain coffee roasters. The farmers gain access to credit, information and
60 farming supplies, enabling them to grow high-quality, often organic coffee for which they receive a decent price. In exchange, consumers get to savour the unbitter taste of coffee that has been 'Fair Trade Certified'.

World Information Society Day

G Today APAEB operates a
85 multimillion-dollar factory
that sells export quality ropes
and rugs to buyers for large
US and European retailers.
From 1997 to 2002, according
90 to Ferreira, annual factory
revenues increased by 400
percent, reaching $6 million,
with three quarters of sales
coming from finished products.
95 The local price for sisal has
tripled, bringing direct economic
benefits to thousands of
families and creating a powerful
economic multiplier effect in
100 a poor region where a million
people earn a part of their
livelihood from sisal. In recent
years dozens of researchers have
visited APAEB to learn how an
105 organization in an isolated rural
area has managed to compete in
the global economy.

Source: David Bornstein *How
to Change the World*, Oxford
University Press, 2007

Glossary

accrue (line 32): to gain
possession (accounting/legal)
alleviate (line 9): to soften
the effects of something
unpleasant
peasant farmer (line 4): a poor
farmer who lives from
subsistence agriculture
pioneer (line 18): to begin or be
at the forefront of something
new, to cross new frontiers
reap (line 78): to harvest
rural peddler (line 4): someone
who sells goods by going from
village to village
urban hawker (line 5): someone
who sells their goods in the
street

E Some social entrepreneurs focus on adding value to productive processes.
A remarkable example is the Associação dos Pequenos Agricultores do
Municipio de Valente (Small Farmers Association of the City of Valente), a
co-operative of sisal farmers known as the APAEB located in the drought-
plagued interior of the Brazilian state of Bahia. (Sisal is an agave plant with
70 lance-shape leaves whose fibers are used to make ropes, rugs, and brushes.)

F In the early 1980s a soft-spoken man named Ismael Ferreira decided that
the economics of sisal farming needed to be changed. The son of a sisal
farmer, Ferreira had spent his childhood working in sun-scorched fields in
a region where most families lived in shacks without electricity or running
75 water. But Ferreira had the opportunity to study accounting and engineering.
And when he returned from school, he no longer would accept an economic
arrangement that kept sisal workers dirt-poor while intermediaries and
manufacturers reaped big profits. Ferreira saw that farmers needed to pool
their output and add value to the sisal before selling it. That meant working
80 together. It took countless meetings to organize the farmers – cooperatives
had a bad reputation in Brazil – and four years of fighting to receive a
government export permit. Eventually, however, the farmers built a brushing
and threshing plant.

E | Critical evaluation

Discuss these questions.

- How neutral is the extract? What is the writer's point of view?
- Does the writer consider any of the disadvantages that 'fair-trade' might bring?
- Which organization has been the most successful in your view?

Business vocabulary

A | International trade collocations

1 Match the words to form collocations from the text.

1	social	a	free
2	informal	b	exposure
3	target	c	resources
4	collateral	d	entrepreneur
5	working	e	economy
6	collective	f	group
7	pool	g	purchasing
8	reduce	h	capital

2 Add collocations from 1 to the gaps in 1–8 and complete the sentences in your own words.

1 Being given a _____-_____ loan has allowed hundreds of thousands of the planet's poorest people _____

2 The _____ _____ for this experiment is people _____

3 It's hard to find a buyer on your own, but if we _____ our _____ we'll _____

4 If you plant several different crops, you'll _____ your _____ to _____

5 A _____ _____ aims to do good by _____

6 If we go for _____ _____ we should be able to save more money _____

7 In some countries the _____ _____ is larger than the _____

8 Without enough _____ _____ it is difficult for businesses _____

B | Compound adjectives: people and places

1 Search the text on page 59 for compound adjectives that describe the following.

Example:

someone who works for himself: self-employed (paragraph A)

1 someone who has very little money: _____ (paragraph F)

2 a place where anything green has been burnt by the sun: _____ (paragraph F)

3 a person who doesn't speak loudly: _____ (paragraph F)

4 a place that suffers from long periods without rain: _____ (paragraph E)

5 a place/thing that cost many millions of dollars to build: _____ (paragraph G)

2 We often used compound adjectives to describe character. Make as many compound adjectives as you can from the words in boxes A and B. Use a dictionary to help you.

hard	even	strong	half
bad	heavy	light	thick
full	fair	small	hot
cold	weak	high	

willed	nosed	handed	tempered
fingered	skinned	minded	headed
hearted	blooded		

3 Complete the sentences with some of the compounds from 2.

1 I wouldn't leave your wallet in your coat, there are some _____ - _____ people around.

2 He says that he is _____ - _____, but in fact he reacts very badly to any kind of criticism.

3 People soon got fed up with her _____ - _____ management style.

4 We are going to launch a _____ - _____ takeover bid, anything less won't work.

5 Don't let the way she looks fool you – she's a _____ - _____ negotiator who will get the best deal she can.

6 Talk to Miriam, she is extremely _____ - _____ and will listen to your side of the story.

4 Create three or four further sentences of your own.

_____

_____

_____

_____

_____

_____

Writing skills

| Improving the content of an essay

1 **Study the essay question. Underline the key words.**

How has the 'fair trade' movement allowed producers from less developed countries to benefit more from their labour and production? What criticisms may be levelled against such initiatives and how justified might they be? Write between 250 and 350 words.

2 **How many questions do candidates have to answer?**

3 **Below are several paragraphs from a draft essay answering the question in 1. Read the paragraphs and the teacher's comments that accompany them.**

1 Match the teacher's comments on each paragraph to one of these categories.

- Structure
- Accuracy
- Cohesion
- Style

2 Is there anything you would add to the teacher's comments?

A Critics of globalization often point to the widening gap between rich and poor countries. It is invariably the role of the poor countries to provide the raw materials and commodities that are in turn processed by their richer customers. If we take a simple jar of instant coffee, the coffee grower receives only a few cents of the final price of the jar. The rest of its added value is divided between merchants and middlemen, transportation, the big brand names that produce their version of coffee, and supermarket chains. Nevertheless, since the advent of free trade the world has certainly become a richer place, so we should be careful before we criticize globalization too heavily.

The paragraph finishes inappropriately – your concluding sentence is not relevant.

_____

_____

B It is common now in the larger supermarkets to see fair trade goods sold alongside the more famous brands. This has provided enormous benefits to small producers in developing countries as they now have the money to invest in village infrastructure such as schools, clinics and hospitals, and housing. Fair trade works in a number of ways. To begin with, it can guarantee that our coffee grower can obtain a fairer price for his production.

This paragraph doesn't have a logical argument. You need to organize it better.

_____

_____

C There are, of course, critical of the fair trade movement. One argument often given against the movement is that it encourages farmers to join a market that is already over-supplied. The reason these commodities have such low prices is that it is already overproduced. Encourage farmers to join the market with fair trade incentives simply saturates the market and lowers everyone's market share.

There are a number of linguistic problems here. Please check thoroughly for language mistakes.

_____

_____

D In my view, it is difficult to level any serious criticism against the free trade movement as it has contributed enormously to improving the lives and prospects of large numbers of people. I feel that its critics are mean-spirited people who want little more than to keep the poorer countries and producers of this world in a neo-colonial framework. I believe that it is virtually now a duty of any right-thinking person to purchase fair trade goods where a choice is made available.

This conclusion is very subjective and personal – not an appropriate tone for an academic essay.

_____

_____

4 **Redraft each paragraph, taking the teacher's comments into consideration.**

Research task

Two organizations that are committed to improving working conditions and getting a fairer deal for workers are *The Rugmark foundation* and *Max Havelaar*. Find out the similarities and differences between these two organizations.

12 Persuasion

Study focus

1 How can advertising agencies be sure that they are reaching the right kind of people?

2 How has advertising changed over the past twenty years?

3 Do you think that consumers are more cynical about advertising than they used to be?

4 Some people claim that they are 'immune' to advertising. How possible is it to be unaffected?

Reading strategies

Look at the definitions of modernism and post-modernism. Can you think of any examples of this from, for example, architecture?

> **modernism:** A style and movement in art, architecture and literature popular in the middle of the 20th century in which modern ideas, methods and materials were used rather than traditional ones.

> **postmodernism:** A style and movement in art, architecture, literature, etc. in the late 20th century that reacts against modern styles, for example by mixing features from traditional and modern styles.

(Definitions taken from *Oxford Advanced Learner's Dictionary* 8th edition)

A | Matching topic sentences

Match sentences 1–7 to the beginnings of paragraphs A–F of the text. There is one extra sentence that you do not need to use.

1 Luxury goods, for example, Prada handbags, Mont Blanc pens, and Vertu's exclusive mobile phone range, are products which sell at very high retail price points.

2 Retro-marketing attempts to induce feelings of pseudo-nostalgia.

3 Whereas modern marketing is concerned with marketing to individual consumers, postmodern marketing is concerned with marketing to 'tribes'; building consumers into communities of consumers.

4 A key feature of postmodern marketing is the development of products and services which feature a new theme on an old product.

5 Brand managers have to think more and more carefully about how to position their products.

6 There is increasingly a belief among consumer researchers that postmodern consumers are incapable of being grouped and segmented according to their needs.

7 Consumption experiences have moved from the satisfaction of mere needs to the realms of the symbolic.

B | Reading for detailed understanding

Choose the correct option.

1 What is not a key feature of post-modern marketing?
   a The creation of meaning in conjunction with consumers.
   b Treating each consumer as a separate entity.
   c Stimulating active participation in the consumption process.
   d Addressing large groups of like-minded consumers.

2 Consumer researchers …
   a are losing confidence in the usual ways of classifying consumers.
   b are heavily influenced by the views of Jean Baudrillard.
   c are confused by the fragmentation and trivialization of people's values.
   d can still easily identify groups with similar needs.

3 How have consumers evolved in postmodern times?
   a They no longer want to be told what they want.
   b Not much – needs fulfilment still comes first.
   c They are fed up with information overload.
   d They are more concerned with a product's values.

4 Marketing on symbolism …
   a is rapidly losing its original power.
   b is most evident in how luxury items are presented.
   c cuts across a wide range of products.
   d is more difficult where services are involved.

5 What has happened to Bibendum, otherwise known as Michelin Man?
   a He is now in his fifth incarnation.
   b He has returned to Michelin's advertisements.
   c He is still loveably fat and round.
   d He has been 'twinned' with the new Mini.

6 The nostalgia generated by retro-marketing …
   a disappoints a product's original consumers.
   b has to appeal to more demanding and sophisticated consumers.
   c re-creates the feeling produced by the original product.
   d is essentially false.

Postmodern marketing

A ___ Whereas modern marketing is concerned with building the image of the company and the brand, postmodern marketers are concerned with building customer experiences. Postmodern marketing
5 emphasizes the value of linking with a product/service rather than simply using it, focusing on co-creation of meaning in its use, rather than simply a transference of meaning from the producer to the consumer. For the postmodern marketer,
10 the consumer actively participates in the brand experience, not simply acting as a passive recipient of advertising messages (see Cova 1996).

B ___ The postmodern consumption era is defined by the celebrated late French cultural critic Jean Baudrillard
15 (1995) as characterized by the fragmentation and trivialization of our values, images and symbols. Fragmentation occurs in everyday life experiences and results in a loss of commitment to a single lifestyle (Firat and Shultz 1997). In these circumstances, the
20 consumer consumes (rather than just purchases), becoming both a customizer and producer of (self-) images in each consumptive experience (Dittmar, 1992; Firat, Dholakia, and Ventakesh, 1995; Gabriel and Lang, 195).

C ___ Consumers are consuming not only the material components of the products but the actual meaning that they represent to them. We shift as consumers, not merely as purchasers from, say, a Shell petrol station, but as purchasers of petrol from a company that we
30 may, or may not, believe is a worthwhile environmental leader. As postmodern consumers, we are (not) buying corporate image and activism, just as much as we are consuming their products.

D ___ They are sold not purely on their functionality
35 but on their aesthetic – visual and sensory – value. The Prada handbag is the epitome of chic, the Mont Blanc pen, the epitome of design and sophistication, and the Vertu phone the epitome of arrival and style. But although we might expect luxury goods to be sold
40 on the basis of their symbolism, there is an increasing shift towards marketing any product on its symbolism. Witness the movement by some companies towards ethical branding e.g. Ben & Jerry's ice cream, the Co-operative Bank, the Body Shop in Britain, and the
45 Italian retailer Benetton. These companies are not merely selling their products, but also their stance on particular issues. For instance, Ben & Jerry's are famous for their positive stance towards the alleviation of world social and environmental problems.
50 The Co-operative Bank has a policy of ethical investment, and so does not bank arms manufacturers, tobacco companies, and other contentious business organizations. Benetton is perhaps the most famous

WAKE UP TO A LITTLE HAPPINESS

HAPPINESS IS 🚗 SHAPED   **Mini**

Austin Morris, a subsidiary of BL Cars.   From Austin Morris with Supercover. 'Mini' is a registered trade mark.

and controversial example, having used high-profile
55 advertisements to raise awareness of social problems in the late 1980s and early 1990s. Similarly, The Body Shop has also embraced, not uncontroversially, the idea of not testing cosmetics on animals (since it was alleged that its suppliers of cosmetic components had tested
60 their products on animals!).

E ___ Brown (2001) defines this as retromarketing or the 'revival or re-launch of a product or service brand from a prior historical period, which is usually, but not always updated to contemporary standards of
65 performance, functioning or taste'. Such examples include the iconic Volkswagen (VW) Beetle re-launched in 1998 and the New Mini, which attempt to recreate and conjure up associations associated with the past for a new set of consumers. More recently, Michelin,
70 the French tyre maker, travel assistance and lifestyle product manufacturer, recast Bibendum, also known as 'Michelin Man' back in its adverts. First created in 1898, Bibendum has gone from being rather overweight in form to being spritely and dynamic in his modern

75 incarnation. Go to http://bibendum-in-museums.
michelin.com/index.htm to see more on Bibendum as
he has evolved over the twentieth century.

ONLY LOVE HANDLES BETTER.

To find out more about MINI's current offers search 'MINI offers'
or text MINI1 to 83338.

Official Fuel Economy Figures for the MINI Range: Urban 27.4 – 67.3 mpg (10.3 – 4.2 l/100km). Extra Urban 45.6 – 80.7 mpg
(6.2 – 3.5 l/100km). Combined 36.7 – 74.3 mpg (7.7 – 3.8 l/100km). CO_2 emissions 180 – 99 g/km.

F ____ We mean this because many consumers may not
have experienced the original brand. So postmodern
80 marketers try to produce an 'authentic' version of
the previous model but enhance it in some way to
bring it into the present. The fact that the product is
really a copy however makes it inauthentic. The fact
that some consumers will not have encountered the
85 original version makes the new version, to that group
of consumers at least, a copy without an original. This
is what Baudrillard (1995) refers to as a simulacrum. A
simulacrum is a copy without an original.

Source: Baine, Fill and Page *Marketing*, Oxford University
Press, 2010

Glossary

activism (line 32): working to achieve political or social change

aesthetic (line 35): connected with notions of beauty and
artistry

contentious (line 52): likely to cause disagreement, or be
the source of argument

epitome (line 36): the perfect example of something

fragmentation (line 15): the breaking up into small pieces

icon (line 66): a symbol, an object of admiration

incarnation (line 75): a form or version of something

nostalgia (page 63): feeling of pleasure and sadness about
the past

pseudo (page 63): a prefix meaning artificial or false

stance (line 46, 48): publicly held opinion/position on an issue

trivialization (line 16): making something seem less
important than it deserves

C | Critical evaluation

Discuss these questions.

- Are 'tribes' really that different from traditional
  groups of consumers?
- To what degree have 'fragmentation' and
  'trivialization' affected our lives?
- How far is the concept of *postmodern marketing* 'old
  wine in new bottles'?
- Of what practical use are Baudrillard's observations?

Business vocabulary

A | Collocations for marketing campaigns

1 Match the words to form collocations from the text.

1	luxury	a	awareness
2	ethical	b	experience
3	raise	c	stance
4	corporate	d	investment
5	advertising	e	advertisement
6	brand	f	goods
7	high-profile	g	message
8	positive	h	image

2 Complete the sentences with the collocations from 1.

1 It is one thing to _____ _____ of a problem and quite another to do something about it.
2 The problem with embracing a policy of _____ _____ is that you may not get the same level of return on your capital.
3 A series of labour scandals tarnished their _____ _____ in the 1990s.
4 I am not sure that our _____ _____ is getting across to consumers. We need to be a lot clearer about what we want to say.
5 Millions of wealthy Asian consumers have given a boost to the market for _____ _____.
6 They grabbed the public's attention with a series of _____ _____ that shocked a lot of people.
7 The company needs to adopt a much more _____ _____ about how it feels about fair trade.
8 We need to come up with new ways of enhancing our customers' _____ _____.

3 Find other marketing collocations that use ...

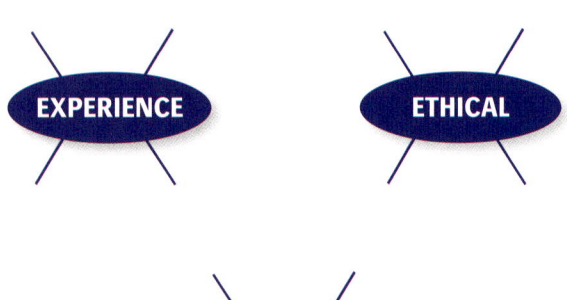

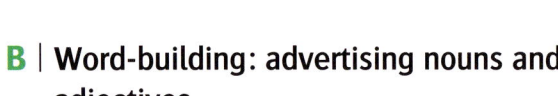

B | Word-building: advertising nouns and adjectives

1 Complete the table.

Noun	Adjective
icon	1
2	nostalgic
3	controversial
contention	4
5	dynamic
ethic	6

2 Continue the sentences in your own words, using the adjectives from 1.

1 Many companies like to demonstrate their _____
_____
2 Their advertising campaign targeting children caused
_____
3 People like to look back at the past _____
_____
4 Their advertisement has become _____
_____
5 Car advertisements often use images that _____
_____
6 The promotion of tobacco related products _____
_____

C | Confusable words

1 Choose the correct option.

1 It was a striking *commercial/advertisement*. People stopped in the street to look at it.
2 The person who designed their world-famous *logo/symbol* was only paid $500.
3 We have conducted research to measure post-transmission *recall/attitude*.
4 There is no point in trying to *target/segment* the market the way we used to. It just doesn't work anymore.
5 Lucinda is the *copywriter/account executive* who is in charge of our top client.
6 A successful *PR/advertising* campaign can get lots of quality reporting in newspapers.
7 I think we should carry out a long-term *market survey/tracking study* to assess the campaign's effectiveness.
8 She came up with the *slogan/message* while she was having a shower.
9 I can't get that stupid *voiceover/jingle* out of my head – it's such a catchy tune.
10 *Viral marketing/Subliminal advertising* was made illegal decades ago,
11 It is one of the high street's best-loved *marks/brands*.
12 Sometimes they hire celebrities to *sponsor/endorse* their products.

2 Write sentences with the words you didn't use.

Writing skills

A | Drafting

1 Look at the steps in writing an essay below. Put the steps in order.

  a Plan your essay. ___
  b Write a first draft. ___
  c Analyse the question. ___
  d Develop research questions. ___
  e Brainstorm your ideas. ___
  f Proof-read your writing. ___
  g Conduct your research. ___
  h Organize your ideas. ___

2 Look at the essay question. Brainstorm your ideas for the essay. Use the text on page 64 to help you.

People do not simply purchase a product to consume it, they also purchase a product because of the values associated with it. To what extent do you agree?

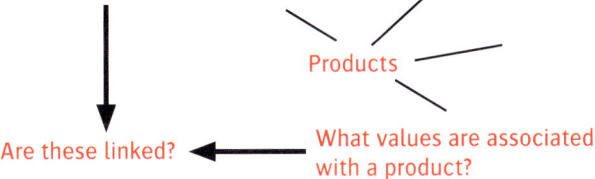

Why do people purchase products?

Products

Are these linked?

What values are associated with a product?

3 Plan your introduction.

  1 Do you mainly agree or disagree with the statement? Try to explain why in one sentence.
  2 What will be your thesis statement?
  3 How could you get the reader's interest on this topic? Write one or two sentences you think gain the reader's interest.

4 Plan the main body.

  1 Organize your ideas into two or three main paragraphs.
  2 Write one topic sentence to show the main idea for each paragraph.
  3 How would you support each idea?
  4 Read the text again and underline parts that might be useful in your essay.
  5 Show the sections you have chosen to a partner and explain why you have chosen them.

5 Plan your conclusion.

  1 What are the main ideas you will need to summarize?
  2 Try to paraphrase your main argument for the conclusion.
  3 Plan your further research questions. What additional information do you need that is not in the text?

B | Revising

1 It is important to thoroughly check your writing after a first draft. Look at the 5 areas below. Think of points you should check for each.

- Introduction
- Paragraphs
- Conclusion
- Language
- Sources

2 Match the questions 1–16 to the areas in 1.

  1 Is no new information mentioned?
  2 Have I used the correct linking phrases?
  3 Is there a balance of direct and indirect quotations?
  4 Is the thesis of the essay clearly restated?
  5 Are the indirect quotes written in my own words?
  6 Is there a topic sentence?
  7 Does it move from general to specific?
  8 Does it give a clear outline of the structure of the essay?
  9 Have I correctly referenced the ideas of others?
  10 Have I checked spelling, sentence structure and word formation?
  11 Does it show a clear line of argument?
  12 Is there a clear summary or logical drawing together of ideas?
  13 Is there a summary, conclusion, or transition?
  14 Does it catch the reader's interest?
  15 Does everything relate to the main idea?
  16 Do the examples clearly and logically support the main idea?

3 What is the most important question you should ask yourself when checking your work? Try to write the one question down.

4 Read the text on page 64 again. Then complete your plan for the essay question in A2 and write at least 500 words on the topic. Use the checklist in B2 to revise and check your drafts.

Research task

1 How do ACORN classifications help companies decide where to send mail-shots or inform how they advertise their products and services?

2 Find out how advertising and PR agencies use tracking studies to assess the effectiveness of their campaigns.

Answer key

Unit 1 Managing globally

Study focus

Answers will vary in this section.

Reading strategies

A | Reading quickly for general understanding

1 c
2 a William James
  b Michael MacAdoo
  c G. Pascal Zachary
  d Michi Sugawar
  e Norbert Luebben

B | Identifying the writer's point of view

1 Companies have become much more international so senior executives are expected to travel more.
2 That they are insufficient – they just deal with superficial differences in culture.
3 Because we can't 100% switch from culture to culture, we can adapt/feel at home in a new culture while retaining our original culture.
4 Our roots are in our birth culture, but we have additional 'winged' cultures when we travel.
5 Because they don't address the fundamental differences about how people in another culture really operate.
6 Because the effort is appreciated by the host country, as in the case of MacAdoo and Chinese culture.
7 They become multi-cultural within themselves.

C | Critical evaluation

Answers will vary in this section.

Business vocabulary

A | Crossing cultures

1 1 c   2 e   3 h   4 a   5 f   6 g   7 i   8 d
  9 b
2 1 paradox   6 insight
  2 smattering   7 host culture
  3 bow   8 cosmopolitan
  4 mindset   9 homogenisation
  5 posting

B | Verbs with prepositions and adverbs

1 1 h   2 e   3 g   4 c   5 f   6 a   7 d   8 b
2 Answers will vary. Suggested answers:
  1 Our service ranges from cultural training … to de-briefing them at the end of their contracts.
  2 The training programme went beyond our expectations.
  3 We need to delve into the reasons why staff don't renew their contracts.
  4 When Gabrielle went to work in New York she left her old self behind.
  5 I am longing for a foreign posting.
  6 Ask her after the lecture, she tends to be more relaxed then.
  7 The recession has cut across all segments of the economy.
  8 It's time we engaged in the problems caused by culture shock.

Writing skills

| Writing a summary

1 1 F   2 T   3 F   4 T   5 F   6 F
2 1 c   2 e   3 b   4 d   5 f   6 a
3 A recent study of 270 CEOs of the companies that comprise <u>Standard and Poors/Toronto Stock Exchange index revealed that 40% had worked outside their home country, up from 29% only a decade ago.</u> <u>The numbers are even higher in Europe.</u> Many companies try t<u>o help executives by offering language courses, relocation training and brief courses on cultural differences.</u> But while these can be useful activities, <u>research suggests that they cannot create the mindset required to survive and thrive in a foreign culture.</u> To achieve this, companies must go much deeper.
4 the writer refers to, although, the writer argues
5 Answers will vary. Suggested answer:
  Paragraph C: Global Manager = person operating successfully across cultures – but person doesn't exist as people are rooted in a culture. 'global' management style doesn't exist. Transcultural executive = someone who can work in two or more cultures.
  Paragraph D: Transcultural managers have roots in one culture but they have 'wings' that mean they can work in other cultures i.e. to have multiple selves. Multiple selves comes from James W in 1890 = people can adapt to various situations
6 Answers will vary. Suggested answer:
  Paragraph C: The author argues that global managers and management do not exist because people's values are rooted in one culture. However, he suggests that a transcultural executive does exist and that this is a person who can work in two or more cultures.
  Paragraph D: The author implies that while people have roots in one culture they can move to other cultures using an alternative self. He quotes the work of James (1890) as the origin of the idea of multiple selves.

Research task

Answers will vary in this section.

Unit 2 Uncertain careers

Study focus

Answers will vary in this section.

Reading strategies

A | Predicting content from topic sentences

1 Answers will vary
2 Answers will vary

B | Reading for detailed understanding

1 F   2 T   3 F   4 T   5 T   6 T   7 F   8 F
9 T   10 T   11 F   12 T

C | Critical evaluation

Answers will vary in this section.

Business vocabulary

A | Key notions: reducing and simplifying

1 1 c   2 e   3 f   4 d   5 a   6 b
2 Answers will vary. Suggested answers:
   1 Working conditions are steadily being eroded.
   2 The person is a victim of 'de-layering'.
   3 The firm has been downsized.
   4 The workforce has been trimmed.
   5 The canteen has been streamlined.

B | Career collocations

managerial/stable CAREER
CAREER satisfaction/expectations/crisis
EMPLOYMENT prospects/relationship
psychological/permanent/fixed-term/part-time/relational
CONTRACT

C | Personal qualities

1 1 b   2 d   3 e   4 a   5 f   6 c
2 They are describing/discussing someone who …
   1 fulfilled their side of the bargain.
   2 has managed to hold down a job, despite an unpromising job history.
   3 is suffering from burn-out.
   4 is willing to go the extra mile.
   5 is intolerant of change.
   6 was upwardly mobile.

Writing skills

| Writing topic sentences

1 Answers will vary. Suggested answer:
   1 It will give an outline of the important changes that occurred in British industrial relations in the 1980s.
   2 It will go into more depth and describe what is normal organizational behaviour.
   3 It will state briefly what it was that made the book so influential and the start of something new.
2 B It is certainly true that in recent years organizations have tried to make the recruitment process more scientific.
   C Large organizations have come to use psychometric tests in order to help them make their choice.
3 Answers will vary. Suggested answer:
   D In the field of graduate recruitment it would appear that graduates are able to predict fairly accurately the aspects of their future job that they will find the easiest or the most difficult.
4 Answers will vary. Suggested answer:
   Despite what has been said, and the considerable evolution in different assessment methods, many organizations still rely on the face to face interview. Whatever its critics may say, the face to face interview is a quick and easy method to decide whether or not the candidate and employer could work together. However, one of the principal drawbacks of the face to face interview is that it has frequently been shown that interviewers have a strong tendency to recruit people who most closely resemble themselves.

Research task

Answers will vary in this section.

Unit 3 Renewing the organization

Study focus

Answers will vary in this section.

Reading strategies

A | Identifying main and supporting ideas

1 1 paragraph C
   2 paragraph A
   3 paragraph E
   4 paragraph B
   5 paragraph D
2 Examples:
   1 Multinationals operate across several countries so they have a more complicated mix of management practices.
   2 Raised awareness of local business market by subsidiaries, e.g. protection, subsidies.
   3 Additional influence of culturally specific value.
3 **Paragraph C**
   Examples of incremental change – incorporation of export department into domestic marketing. Develops idea and says incremental change is the role of management.
   Paragraph D
   Contrasts incremental change with transformational change. Focuses on leadership. Contrasts different views of leadership across different cultures.
   Paragraph E
   Considers difficulties of managing change in multinational companies. Cites research by Harding that contrasts how change was dealt with at plants in Germany and Britain.

B | Reading for detailed understanding

1 b   2 a   3 d   4 b   5 c

C | Critical evaluation

Answers will vary in this section.

Business vocabulary

A | Organizational change

1 1 h   2 e   3 j   4 i   5 f   6 a   7 c   8 d
   9 b   10 g
2 1 incorporate   2 sanctioned   3 piecemeal
   4 undertook   5 inherent   6 hindered   7 overcome
   8 incremental   9 empowering   10 underpinned

B | Verbs with over-, under-

1 undervalued; underpaid   2 overtime   3 underlying
4 overdue   5 overhauled   6 undertaking   7 overview
8 overheads   9 underwritten   10 oversight

C | Opposite meanings

1 1 The CEO tabled the suggestion. (meaning 3b)
   2 It was an oversight. (meaning 1a)
   3 New sanctions in the form of fines have been introduced. (meaning 2a)
   4 Angry shareholders are going to table a motion. (meaning 3a)
   5 The multi-billion dollar project has been sanctioned. (meaning 2b)
   6 A committee of experts has been given oversight of deep water drilling activities. (meaning 1b)

2 **1** The British speaker thinks that when the board agreed to table his proposal that they wanted to hear more. In fact, 'table' in US English means to postpone.

2 The US speaker thinks he was talking about who would have 'oversight'; i.e. overall responsibility and supervision, when his British counterparts thought that he was talking about an oversight; i.e. a mistake.

3 The speaker doesn't understand which use of sanction is meant.

Writing skills

A | Paragraph features

1 **1** a, c, d, e

2 b, f

2 (d) Strategic change in multinationals is more complex than that in single-country firms. (e) The more complex the environment within which change takes place, the more difficult it is to design and implement a coherent change strategy. (a) Multinational firms are companies that operate across several countries, which creates a complex and sometimes chaotic mélange of management practices influenced by different national cultures and institutions. (c) In addition, some subsidiaries are more aware of the competitive nature of the business environment, perhaps because of the subsidiary or the industry is protected or subsidized by the government, and hence may not understand the importance of change and resist it. (e) Further, people's attitudes towards change are also affected by a set of culture-specific factors, such as taken for granted behaviour, norms and values, which adds another layer of complexity to change management in multinational firms. (b) The different behaviours and attitudes of employees and management at subsidiary level towards change increase the potential for conflict between the centre and subsidiaries, and may hinder the success of the change strategy (Andrews and Chompusri 2001).

Feature f is not included

B | Paragraph structure

1 **1** c, a, b, e, d

2 c, b, f, a, e, d

2 Answers will vary. Suggested answer:

Paragraph 1: Succession handovers can be challenging in any firm but particularly so in a family-run business. Family firms often struggle, at times of transition, to move out of the control of the founder. They have exerted influence not only over the company but also the other family members. When there is not one clear individual for the firm to be passed onto this can add further problems to the situation. Issues such as jealousy and interference from other family members can impact on the success of the transition.

Paragraph 2: Depending on whom the successor is they will face a number of challenges. For an inexperienced successor there could be more problems with other family members and staff that perhaps do not have faith in their knowledge and ability. Alternatively, the successor may have very different plans or expectations from the founder and consequently find it challenging to gain the support of staff. All of these factors can lead to disillusionment or a lack of respect for the new leader.

Paragraph 3: Whilst there are clearly a number of issues facing inter-generational successors there are a number of tactics that can be used to mitigate them. Firstly, it would be valuable for the successor to gain experience from outside the family firm before taking over. Such a tactic may enable the successor to more easily gain the respect of employees or other family members. Secondly, careful planning so that the change is gradual and not sudden will enable everyone to adapt more effectively to the new situation. Finally, it should be remembered that if there is no worthwhile successor from within the family then appointing an external candidate should be considered.

3 Answers will vary

4 Answers will vary. Suggested answer:

There are two main types of change a company faces; incremental change and transformational change. Incremental change is generally considered to be small and to have little impact on the core values of an organization. They are the type of changes introduced by managers which are mainly aimed at increases in efficiency. On the other hand, transformational changes involve changing the fundamental beliefs and values of an organization. Transformational change requires strong leadership from the top as it impacts on the very basis on which a company has been built.

Research task

Answers will vary in this section.

Unit 4 Ensuring good behaviour

Study focus

Answers will vary in this section.

Reading strategies

A | Using background knowledge to understand content

1 Answers will vary

2 Answers will vary

B | Reading for general understanding

1 a is the closest description

C | Reading for detailed understanding

1 **1** How can people find out about the financial health of a business/How can people find out if a business is a suitable place for them to invest their money?

2 How do they know they can trust the information in the published accounts?

3 Do the accounts cover everything/every aspect of the business' activities?

4 Who is affected when a company fails/goes bankrupt?

5 What is the best way of protecting investors and making sure that they have the best available information?

2 **1** Enron **2** Barings **3** Barings **4** Enron
5 Barings **6** Barings **7** Enron **8** Enron

3 Answers will vary

D | Reading for inference

Suggested answers:
1 Because he had been the bank's 'golden boy' and they believed he could do no wrong.
2 He had probably gambled on futures in shares and currency.
3 When the bank agreed to send more money. If they had uncovered his wrongdoing then they would have lost an enormous amount of money but they might have survived.
4 As an old and established bank they may not have been entirely familiar with the instruments that Leeson was using. Or quite simply they trusted in his judgement too much.
5 A combination of senior management and Andersen.
6 No, she specifically states that they were set up to conceal payments. What should have been a third party hedge gave no protection at all to investors.
7 Andersen was probably so scared of losing such a lucrative account that they were willing to go along with anything that Enron demanded.
8 Because senior figures were so busy lining their own pockets with money that had been siphoned off from the company through the SPEs.

E | Note-taking

Answers will vary. Suggested answer:
Barings – Nick Leeson – Enron CEO
Leeson was poorly supervised so people knew little about what was going on until it was too late. It seems that lots of people benefited from the wrong-doing at Enron. The Barings collapse happened over a matter of a few months. With Enron the wrongdoing had gone on for many years. The warning signals at Barings came too late to do anything about it, while at Enron people ignored the warnings of a whistleblower high up in the company. At Barings there was little supervision/governance while at Enron its outside auditors were implicated in the cover up.

F | Critical evaluation

Answers will vary in this section.

Business vocabulary

A | Company finance

1 1 auditor 2 collapse 3 board 4 exposure
   5 hedge 6 integrity 7 lucrative 8 sound
   9 shareholders 10 whistleblower 11 takeover bid
   12 bankruptcy
2 1 auditor 2 lucrative 3 sound 4 bankruptcy
   5 takeover bid 6 hedge 7 exposure 8 integrity
   9 board 10 whistleblower 11 shareholders
   12 collapse

B | Phrasal verbs for corporate governance

1 1 b 2 j 3 f 4 c 5 h 6 i 7 d 8 a
   9 g 10 e
2 cause – bring about
   establish – set up
   fail to happen – fall through
   submit a request –file for
   conceal the truth – cover up
   cancel – write off
   wait and see – hold back
   avoid – get around
   rescue – bail out
   restore order – sort out

Writing skills

A | Connecting and contrasting ideas

1 2 contrast: although, since, while, conversely, despite, nevertheless, however, whereas, even though
   3 related examples: in addition, furthermore, besides, moreover
   4 cause and effect: results in, because, leads to, due to, contributes to, hence, thus, consequently, therefore
   5 similarities: likewise, similarly
2 1 moreover, however
   2 thus
   3 likewise, however
   4 despite, thus
   5 results in
3 1 nevertheless
   2 thus
   3 hence
   4 even though
   5 whereas

B | Writing practice

1 Answers will vary
2 Answers will vary. Suggested answer:
   Parmalat is an Italian company famous for its long-life milk. It was at the centre of a financial scandal and has been called the Italian Enron. Founded by businessman Calisto Tanzi, like Enron, it seemed to be a remarkable success story. However, when in 2003 the firm was unable to make a bond payout the truth came out and investors realized that the company did not have enough money in its reserves to meet its obligations. Tanzi had covered up the firm's losses through fraudulent accounting and using money from new investors to pay existing ones. Consequently the firm collapsed, enormous debts of 13 billion pounds were revealed – the largest number of victims were the many thousands of small investors who thought that they couldn't lose. A three-year trial resulted in Tanzi being finally sentenced to eighteen years in jail and his art collection being seized. Nevertheless, none of this was enough to pay back the money owing to small investors.

Research task

Answers will vary in this section.

Unit 5 Motivation

Study focus

Answers will vary in this section.

Reading strategies

A | Scanning for specific information

1 MHT = Motivator-Hygiene Theory
   JCM = Job Characteristics Model
   JDS = Job Diagnostic Survey
   GNS = growth need strength
2 MHT: Frederick Herzberg
   JCM, JDS, GNS: Hackman and Oldham

B | Reading and note-taking

MHT = motivator-hygiene theory
motivator factors: intrinsic to job – responsibility, achievement, recognition
hygiene factors: associated with job – work setting, relationship with peers, subordinates, supervision, wage/salary

JCM = job characteristics model
core job characteristics:
1 skill variety refers to the number of skills needed for job
2 task identity refers to whether does the job requires completion
3 task significance refers to the job's impact on others
4 autonomy refers to the employees' level of freedom/independence and discretion
5 job feedback refers to clear information about performance
3 psychological states:
a experienced meaningfulness of work
b experienced responsibility for work outcomes
c knowledge of work results

C | Reading for detailed understanding

1 Making workers specialize on one task and simplifying it to achieve maximum efficiency.
2 Workers reacted with lateness (tardiness), falling motivation and productivity and sabotage.
3 Motivator factors are intrinsic to the job; hygiene factors are associated with the job.
   Examples:
   motivator factors: responsibility, achievement, recognition, personal growth in competence.
   hygiene factors: relationship with peers and subordinates, quality of supervision, base wage/salary.
4 There is a lack of differentiation between factors. A pay rise could be both a motivator and hygiene factor.
5 It builds on it.
6 The three psychological states are influenced by the five core job characteristics.
7 People with high GNS seek out challenging jobs and are satisfied with the supervision they receive; and with their co-workers.
8 They largely appear to support them.
9 The connection is not totally clear. The analysis of research has given conflicting results. Tiegs Tetrick and Fried's claim that their research fails to show the link between high GNS and motivation; but a re-examination of the same research data by other experts claim it does.

D | Critical evaluation

Answers will vary in this section.

Business vocabulary

A | Performance and job satisfaction

1 1 enhance
   2 intrinsic
   3 autonomy
   4 enrich
   5 absenteeism
   6 accomplish
   7 competence
   8 sabotage
   9 adverse consequences

2 1 enhanced
   2 intrinsic
   3 autonomously
   4 competent
   5 accomplish

3 1 The introduction of new equipment enhanced staff satisfaction and lent more meaningfulness.
   2 Encouraging staff autonomy lent more validity to their efforts.
   3 This had the additional effect of enhancing their motivation and their relationship with supervisors.

B | Key notions: thoughts and ideas

1 1 d   2 c   3 e   4 f   5 a   6 b
2 1 approach
   2 hypothesis
   3 theory
   4 premise
   5 theory
   6 models
3 1 hypothesis
   2 hypothesize
   3 hypothetical
   4 hypothetically
   5 hypotheses

Writing skills

| Paraphrasing other people's ideas

1 1 Wrong – only cite the ideas of the original
   2 Correct
   3 Correct
   4 Wrong – use your own words
   5 Wrong – not unless you are writing a critical summary
   6 Correct
   7 Wrong – use synonyms, re-phrase
   8 Correct

2 Single source: a, c, e, g, j, k
   Multiple sources: b, d, f, h, i,

3 The following section should be underlined:
   For instance, neither Wahba nor Bridewell have found concrete evidence to support this proposition, while Manfred Max-Neef argues that basic human needs are non-hierarchical and cannot be neatly separated out as Maslow suggests. Furthermore, Geert Hofstede, the Dutch social psychologist and anthropologist, criticizes Maslow's theory as being ethnocentric.

4 a However, research has revealed that the routine and standardized tasks associated with the 'scientific management' approach have led to a number of unintended adverse consequences.
   b These new approaches focused on the motivation of employees at work as a key determinant of job attitude and performance.
   c Frederick W Taylor, who was the first to focus on job design for individuals, developed the 'scientific management' approach in 1911.
   d Taylor's approach focused on specialization and simplification of jobs as mechanisms to enhance efficiency and control performance

e … such as higher tardiness, lower motivation and productivity, and sabotage of work equipment. This meant that the gains made in the industrial engineering approach were often overshadowed by its negative effects.

5 Answers will vary

6 Answers will vary. Suggested answers:

1 McClelland argues that what motivates individuals is determined by their underlying character. Thus, their innate personality will determine which of three motivating factors they will respond to. In some instances individuals may be motivated by the need for power and to be the focal point of attention. For others, the need for affiliation, that is a sense of belonging and the acknowledgement of others, may be paramount. While for the third group it may be the need for achievement and a terror of failure that motivates them.

2 Vroom argues that people's actions are determined by how advantageous they believe their results. Their performance is in direct proportion to their perception of the attractiveness of the end result. Hence, the theory concentrates on the connection between performance and gain and the successful realization of individual goals.

3 J.Stacey Adam's 'Equity Theory' argues that motivation is determined by how individuals measure their rewards in comparison with others. The effort they expend and the benefits they reap need to be in line with the efforts and gains of others. If this is deemed to be unfair it will have an adverse effect on their performance. This may in turn lead to a reduction in the quantity of their work or indeed their resignation.

Research task

Answers will vary in this section.

Unit 6 Culture

Study focus

Answers will vary in this section.

Reading strategies

A | Brainstorming ideas

1 strategy – a plan, often longer term
multinational enterprise – a business with branches and subsidiaries in other countries.

2 Answers will vary

B | Scanning for specific information

1 b   2 e   3 f   4 d   5 c   6 a

C | Reading for detailed understanding

1 1 To find new markets.
2 They become saturated.
3 Because the firm can use unused resources, including managerial 'know-how'.
4 Because firms generally start to look abroad from early on; they don't wait for saturation of the domestic market to occur.
5 They benefit from economies of scale and become more adept at learning. Being bigger gives them more market power when they are buyers.
6 They become more efficient and benefit from economies of scale that allow them to dominate rivals who are smaller and less widespread.

7 a Sony and Honda were 'second tier' firms in Japan, so they went to the US where they didn't face this competition.
b They were able to access cutting edge developments in engine technology.
c They were able to acquire local 'smartcard' technology that was unavailable in the US.

8 They can adapt research and development and technology according to the requirements of local markets.

2 1 It has evolved from protecting them at all costs to allowing them to be disseminated more widely. The old model saw the dissemination of FSRCs as losing competitive advantage.

2 Advantages: Firm retains know-how. Can use this know-how for its own competitive advantage.
Disadvantages: Restricted reach. Will encourage local competitors to come up with their own solutions to problems. Will stimulate competition.

3 Because by doing so it allows firms to diversify their markets and stop the need for local competitors to imitate or pirate the product.

D | Critical evaluation

Answers will vary in this section.

Business vocabulary

A | Organizational strategy

1 1 e   2 f   3 c   4 a   5 b   6 d
2 1 cutting edge
2 income stream
3 competitive advantage
4 joint venture
5 intellectual property
6 learning curve
3 1 intellectual property
2 joint venture
3 cutting edge
4 income stream
5 learning curve
6 competitive advantage
4 Answers will vary

B | Collocations with 'market'

1 domestic, national, international, wide-ranging, home, American, local, foreign, market power
2 Answers will vary. Suggested answers:
buyer's/seller's/leader/niche/penetration/research/segment/share/price
3 Answers will vary

C | Organizational strategy word-building

1 1 acquisition
2 managerial (management)
3 theoretical
4 Diversification
5 Geographically
6 innovative
7 internationalization
8 opportunistic
9 accessible
10 globalization

2 **1** noun   **2** adj   **3** adj   **4** noun   **5** adv   **6** adj
    7 noun   **8** adj   **9** adj   **10** noun

3 acquire oO acquisition ooOo
    manager Ooo managerial ooOoo
    theory Ooo theoretical ooOoo
    diversify oOoo diversification ooooOo
    geography oOoo geographically ooOoo
    innovate Ooo innovative Oooo
    international ooOo internationalization oooooOoo
    opportunity ooOoo opportunistic oooOo
    access Oo accessible oOoo
    global Oo globalization oooOo

Writing skills

A | Question analysis

1 **a** benefits of free trade + ever any justification for
       protectionism
    b benefits of free trade = description
       justification for protectionism = evaluation

2 **1** d   **2** a   **3** b   **4** e   **5** f   **6** c

3 **a** China
    b 21st century

B | Planning and organizing an essay

1 Answers will vary

2 Answers will vary

3 The examples in 2 could be organized into:
    Paragraph 1: benefits to consumers – price and choice
    Paragraph 2: benefits to companies – earn more money from an
    increased market, trade is cheap e.g. less taxes, trade is quicker
    due to less bureaucracy
    Paragraph 3: benefits of protectionism to consumers – salaries
    may be protected and job security higher
    Paragraph 4: benefits of protectionism for national companies
    – less competition, no restrictions on export, more security for
    protected companies

4 Answers will vary

5 Answers will vary

Research task

Answers will vary in this section.

Unit 7 Organizational learning

Study focus

Answers will vary in this section.

Reading strategies

A | Understanding the relationship between text and graphic

1 12 o'clock – generate
    3 o'clock – integrate
    6 o'clock – interpret
    9 o'clock – act

2 **1** R&D must not be isolated from everything else but be
       conducted by line management.
    2 Employees must be multi-skilled and multi-functioning; i.e.
       not stuck in a single role.
    3 Information should be discussed with an open mind. Should
       not be 'funnelled' to a conclusion.
    4 Everyone should be on a far more equal basis. Less
       hierarchy, more open and frank discussion.

B | Reading for general understanding

b

C | Reading for detailed understanding

Paragraph C

1 Supportive organization structure and culture.

2 In 'functional chimneys' with specialization in different areas of
    the business. Managers were interested in pursuing their own
    ambitions or the goals of their group rather than thinking about
    the overall good of the company.

3 **a** People didn't talk to people in other departments.
    b Suspicion and rivalry.

4 Intense competition from Asian manufacturers.

Paragraph D

1 Their costs were too high and their time-scales too long.

2 Japanese companies were more integrated and cross-functional.

3 It owned 25% of Mazda so it could access its management
    know-how.

4 The four pillars are:
    1 communication between product development and
       manufacturing
    2 formal co-operation (between departments) and cross-
       functional careers
    3 team culture and shared responsibility
    4 customer-driven processes

5 **a** To introduce cross-functional career paths.
    b To increase lateral communication; i.e. between departments.

D | Summarizing

Towards the end of the 1980s Ford Europe was facing trouble
because of foreign competition, mainly from Asia. It also had
high costs and long lead time. The problems emanated from
how the company was organized which led to a culture of
interdepartmental rivalry and mangers pursuing their own goals.
The company's management realized that they had to make
radical changes quickly. Luckily for Ford it had a 25% share
in Mazda so was able to tap into what the Japanese company
did. From Mazda it learned that there needed to be a change in
culture that included cross functional careers, discussion and the
introduction of simultaneous engineering that required people
from different departments to speak to each other. Accordingly, the
company introduced the following changes: it made careers more
cross-functional and adopted policies to reduce interdepartmental
rivalry and encourage communication.

E | Critical evaluation

Answers will vary in this section.

Business vocabulary

A | Learning processes

1 **1** experiential learning
    2 concrete experience
    3 reflective observation
    4 abstract conceptualization
    5 active experimentation
    6 drawing conclusions

2 Our company is committed to the principle of experiential
    learning and basing its findings on concrete experience.
    Following a period of reflective observation, and abstract
    conceptualization we will actively experiment with what we
    have learnt before drawing firm conclusions.

B | Departments in organizations
a accounts
b finance
c marketing
d personnel (human resources)
e R&D
f manufacturing (production)

C | Verbs to describe experimental processes
1 1 j   2 d   3 f   4 a   5 h   6 b   7 e   8 i
    9 c   10 g
2 a emerge, transpire
   b determine
   c test out
   d reflect on, hypothesize
   e draw the conclusion
   f instil
   g ascertain, infer, deduce
3 Answers will vary in this section.

Writing skills

A | Opening and closing paragraphs
1 1 d   2 a   3 e   4 c   5 b
2 1 a   2 e   3 c   4 b
3 1 i   2 h   3 j   4 g   5 f
4 We can see that by and large it treats each of the points in term.

B | Useful language
1 a Saying what you intend to do
   b Defining and narrowing
   c Stating what you have done
2 Answers will vary
3 Answers will vary

Research task
Answers will vary in this section.

Unit 8 Financing business

Study focus
1 Primary: mining, farming, forestry, fishing
Manufacturing: car-making, steel-making, textiles, shipbuilding
Services: Retail, banking, hospitals, education, insurance
2 Answers will vary
3 Answers will vary

Reading strategies

A | Using background knowledge to predict content
1 Answers will vary
2 1 helps provide money for business
   2 facilitates international payment transactions
   3 buying and selling of raw material
   4 covers different kinds of risk
   5 trades in financial products such as options and futures

B | Reading for detailed understanding
1 Direct investment involves putting money directly into a company. Portfolio investment involves buying a range of shares in different businesses using 'surplus capital'. What is of interest is making a return.

2 They sold bundles of derivatives that contained high levels of sub-prime mortgage debt. The loans had been 'securitised' as sold on to financial institutions that probably had a poor understanding of their eventual exposure. When US borrowers defaulted on their loans this had a domino effect on everybody who had bought these derivatives.

3 Financial markets are much faster and reactive to events.

4 Traders look out for small differences in values across markets and move vast sums of money to profit from them.

5 It is inefficient.

6 They are all fully convertible currencies that are allowed to float freely and realize their market value.

7 It was extremely volatile.

8 It made life difficult because buyers and sellers on each side of the Atlantic couldn't have the confidence that a stable exchange rate brings.

9 Rates were fixed. It brought stability and international trade prospered.

10 Most currencies float. If a country has a trade deficit this will eventually be reflected in the value of the currency which find its true level. (Of course this does not work for the euro that has been adopted by many different economies in the EU and has led stronger members having to 'bail out' its weaker partners)

C | Critical evaluation
Answers will vary in this section.

Business vocabulary

| Financial vocabulary
1 1 arbitrage   2 asset   3 bond   4 commodity
    5 depreciation   6 default   7 derivative   8 hedge
    9 mortgage   10 portfolio   11 security   12 stock
2 1 divide up someone's portion
   2 keep goods to sell
   3 keeping safe
   4 a plant division between two fields or gardens
   5 understand the value/worth of something
   6 something that ties two things together
   7 a selection of an artist's work, a kind of briefcase
3 1 fencing – hedging
   2 assets – commodities
   3 arbitration – arbitrage
   4 defected – defaulted
   5 shares – bonds
   6 deviations – derivatives
   7 security guard – securities trader

Writing skills

| Incorporating sources
1 A uses the exact words, 'quotation marks', the author's surname, year of publication and page number. B uses the ideas but different words, the author's surname and year of publication.
2 An indirect quote uses the ideas from a text expressed in an original way. The source is referenced by giving only the year and author surname.

3 **1** The value of a currency can change rapidly and have a major impact on the costs of importing and export.

2 illustrates

3 As Henderson (1999) illustrates, the euro on its launch was worth $1.18 but just under two years later it was valued at 0.84c. Just over 4 years later it had risen to $1.34.

4 Such changes will have a significant impact on a company's ability to export and also the cost of any imports. Such factors, that lay outside a company's control, make international markets very volatile to trade in.

4 b

5 Answers will vary. Suggested answer:

One challenge can be when a currency covers a number of countries such as the euro. Countries with a deficit are hindered when a currency remains strong due to the economic power of other member states.

OR

Consequently a country may be able to export its way out of recession.

6 Answers will vary. Suggested answer:

A financial crisis can often lead to calls for changes such as stronger financial regulation, market liberalisation or currency controls. As Henderson (2009) states the call for greater financial regulation was particularly strong in 2008-9 in order to avert similar financial disasters in the future. The demand for regulation was largely based on the fact that the financial crisis stemmed from the actions of financial institutions.

7 Answers will vary

Research task

Answers will vary in this section.

Unit 9 Product life cycles

Study focus

Answers will vary in this section.

Reading strategies

A | Predicting content from a diagram
1 Answers will vary
2 Answers will vary

B | Reading for general understanding
b

C | Reading for detailed understanding
1 **a** phase 2
   b phase 4
   c phase 1
2 1 F   2 NG   3 F   4 F   5 NG   6 T   7 NG
   8 T
3 **1** It can be used to plan. For example, new products/extensions may be introduced in a mature market.
   2 It may be an entirely new product in some markets.
   3 It may be difficult to assess market share. In this case, it will be hard to decide which strategy to adopt.
   4 It can help a firm to decide its investment priorities.
   5 They follow the undulating curve of the building industry – peaks and troughs.

D | Critical evaluation
Answers will vary in this section.

Business vocabulary

A | Formal verbs
1 alleviate – relieve/make something less severe
cease – stop
emanate – come from
embark – begin something new or difficult
enhance – improve
inform – influence/affect
occur – happen
solicit – ask for
surge – increase suddenly
thrive – do lots of business/be successful

2 **1** Since we discovered where these problems emanated from we have been able to alleviate the damage done.

2 Before we embark on a mass production programme we need to ensure that these problems do not (re-) occur.

3 We do not need to cease production but to enhance sales in new markets.

4 A continued surge in interest rates will inform our production costs.

5 Since they solicited our help their company has thrived.

B | Nominalization
1 1 consumption   2 strength   3 expenditure
   4 restraint   5 retention   6 growth   7 criticism
   8 elimination   9 extension
2 Answers will vary

C | Homographs
1a object (verb) when you don't agree with something
2b object (noun) topic/subject
2a present (verb) to show everyone
2b present (noun) gift
3a appropriate (verb) to take/acquire
3b appropriate (adj) suitable
4a content (adj) satisfied
4b content (noun) what is included
5a closer (comparative adjective) nearer
5b closer (noun) someone who knows how to make a deal

Writing skills

A | Problem solution essays
1 Answers will vary
2 Answers will vary
3 Answers will vary

B | Evaluative language
1 1 flawed, only
   2 whilst … interesting … lacks proof
   3 only addresses, inadequate
   4 unfortunately … insufficient data
   5 effective tool
   6 clearly addresses
   7 likely to resolve
2 1 resolve
   2 flawed
   3 lacks proof
   4 inadequate/insufficient
   5 inadequate/insufficient
   6 clearly addresses
   7 effective

C | Writing practice

1 1 b   2 d   3 a   4 c

2 Answers will vary

Research task

Answers will vary in this section.

Unit 10 Leadership

Study focus

Answers will vary in this section.

Reading strategies

A | Skimming for gist

Λ 2   B 1   C 2   D 1

B | Scannning for specific information

1 Vroom and Jago
2 Murphy
3 Ruth
4 Meindl & Ehrlich
5 Krohe
6 Bennis
7 Bligh and Meindl
8 Schriesheim
9 Carmeli and Schaubroeck
10 McNatt
11 Padilla, Hogan and Kaiser

C | Reading for detailed understanding

1 It seems to provide answers to the problems that organizations face.
2 Just in people's minds. It is ultimately 'an abstract concept'.
3 It makes them less susceptible to being naïve, and confusing what they think (perceive) with what is true (reality).
4 Romantic leadership, i.e. the leader as a heroic figure.
5 They don't take into account 'the situational variables', i.e. the conditions and constraints in which firms and leaders exist, and which in turn can determine outcomes.
6 It deals with how heroic leaders overcome difficulties to achieve success.
7 Followers traditionally are 'powerless, passive and predictable'. Evidence suggests that this is not always the case as followers may oppose or try to isolate their leaders.
8 By making people have belief in themselves, i.e. if your leader/boss has belief in you, you will have belief in yourself.
9 If a boss/leader has low or negative expectations of someone, they will tend to fulfil them.
10 That the influence they have on each other is two-way.

D | Critical evaluation

Answers will vary in this section.

Business vocabulary

A | Adjectives to describe leaders and followers

1 1 c   2 a   3 f   4 g   5 b   6 h   7 d   8 e

2 1 proactive   2 heroic   3 romantic   4 naïve
   5 compliant   6 passive   7 predictable   8 conformist

B | Word-building: negative prefixes

1 dis: disproportionate, disentangling
   in: inexhaustible
   mis: no examples
   ir: no examples
   il: no examples
   un: unpredictable, unrealistically

2 1 unscientific, illogical
   2 impatience, unpredictability, unpopularity
   3 disentanglement, irreproachability
   4 Unreasonable, disloyalty
   5 inexhaustible
   6 irrespective
   7 untrustworthy, illegal
   8 unrealistic, unachievable
   9 immature, disproportionate
   10 miscalculation, undoing

C | Synonyms

1 conviction, belief, opinion
   element, factor
   outcome, result
   perspective, viewpoint, perception
   robust, strong
   idea, notion, concept
   focal point, focus
   goal, target

2 1 c   2 a   3 d   4 e   5 b

3 Answers will vary

Writing skills

A | Presenting opinions: introductory adverbs

1 1 Regrettably   2 Consequently   3 Personally
   4 Admittedly   5 Understandably   6 Hopefully
   7 Clearly   8 Accordingly

B | Presenting opinions: modifying adverbs

1 1 It is entirely understandable why people seek advice from books.
2 They may feel totally unprepared to assume a leadership role themselves.
3 However, I found the ideas contained in this guide deeply depressing.
4 Unfortunately, its assertions are completely unsupported by scientific evidence.
5 Sadly, readers' reviews appear to agree wholeheartedly with any outrageous suggestion.
6 Nevertheless, in my view, its publishers should apologize profusely for printing such complete nonsense.

C | Approaching essays

1 1 The writer believes that leadership is innate and dissaproves of leadership books.
2 The writer uses quite a lot of vocabulary that carries a negative connotation. E.g. seduce, cutthroat, cynicism, false-hope merchants etc.

2 Answers will vary

Research task

Answers will vary in this section.

Unit 11 Doing good by doing business

Study focus
Answers will vary in this section.

Reading strategies

A | Predicting content from an introduction
1 One of the main criticisms is poor working conditions in factories and labour abuses. This cannot apply to most poor workers as they are self-employed.
2 Social entrepreneurs try to address the question of how the poor can maximize the benefits they receive from their work.
3 Answers will vary

B | Identifying main ideas
1 F   2 G   3 B   4 C   5 D

C | Reading for general information

Organization/ Founder	Where it works	Its focus	Who it helps	How it helps
Grameen bank. Founder: Mohammad Yunus	Bangladesh	Providing people with small collateral-free loans.	The poor who would not otherwise be able to borrow money. Mostly women workers.	Helps women generate additional income so they can improve their lives and the lives of their families.
SEWA Founder: Ela Bhatt	India	Improving market relations.	Self-employed poor women.	By forming them into a powerful trade union. This protects workers and promotes favourable government policies.
WESA Founder: Gisèle Yitamben	Cameroon	Making markets accessible.	Small businesswomen; fruit growers, craftswomen, translators.	Uses the Internet to put producers in direct contact with buyers.
TransFair Founder: Paul Rice	From USA	"	Small coffee growers.	Links growers with major US retailers.
APAEB Founder: Ismael Ferreira	Brazil	Adding value to sisal production.	Sisal farmers	Building value into Sisal production by producing finished products for export, rather than simply exporting raw sisal.

D | Reading for detail and for inference
1 It is how value is added at each stage of processing. For instance, value is added to coffee by roasting and grinding, brewing, freeze-drying and packing, transport, marketing and retailing. At each step of the way value is added.
2 Because they wouldn't be able to provide 'collateral', i.e. a guarantee against non-payment of a loan.
3 It enables people to improve their standard of living.
4 It is for women.
5 The Internet can be used to put producers in direct contact with buyers.

6 It has had a 'multiplier effect'. In other words the money it generates supports a wider economy.
7 How to make cooperatives work.
8 The writer obviously admires him, considers him a hero.

E | Critical evaluation
Answers will vary in this section.

Business vocabulary

A | International trade collocations
1 1 d   2 e   3 f   4 a   5 h   6 g   7 c   8 b
2 1 collateral free
   2 target group
   3 pool resources
   4 reduce exposure
   5 social entrepreneur
   6 collective purchasing
   7 informal economy
   8 working capital

B | Compound adjectives: people and places
1 1 dirt-poor   2 sun-scorched   3 soft-spoken
   4 drought-plagued   5 multimillion-dollar
2 hard-nosed, hard-headed, hard-hearted, even-handed, even-tempered, strong-willed, half-hearted, bad-tempered, heavy-handed, light-fingered, thick-skinned, full-blooded, fair-minded, small-minded, hard-headed, hard-hearted, hot-tempered, hot-headed, hot-blooded, cold-heated, cold-blooded, weak-willed , high-handed, high-minded
3 1 light-fingered   2 thick-skinned
   3 heavy-handed/high-handed   4 full-blooded
   5 hard-headed   6 fair-minded

Writing skills

| Improving the content of an essay
1 Answers will vary
2 3
3 1 A cohesion   B structure   C accuracy   D style
   2 Answers will vary.
4 Answers will vary

Research task
Answers will vary in this section.

Unit 12 Persuasion

Study focus
Answers will vary in this section.

Reading strategies

A | Matching topic sentences
A 3   B 6   C 7   D 1   E 4   F 2
5 is the extra and unnecessary sentence

B | Reading for detailed understanding
1 b   2 a   3 d   4 c   5 b   6 d

C | Critical evaluation
Answers will vary in this section.

Business vocabulary

A | Collocations for marketing campaigns

1 1 f   2 d   3 a   4 h   5 g   6 b   7 e   8 c

2 1 raise awareness   2 ethical investment
   3 corporate image   4 advertising message
   5 luxury goods   6 high-profile advertisements
   7 positive stance   8 brand experience

3 Answers will vary. Suggested answer:
   customer experience, life experience, consumptive experience,
   ethical branding, ethical goods, ethical shopping, service brand,
   original brand, top brand

B | Word-building: advertising nouns and adjectives

1 1 iconic   2 nostalgia   3 controversy   4 contentious
   5 dynamism   6 ethical

2 Answers will vary

C | Confusable words

1 1 advertisement   2 logo   3 recall   4 segment
   5 account executive   6 PR   7 tracking study
   8 slogan   9 jingle   10 Subliminal advertising
   11 brands   12 endorse

2 Answers will vary

Writing skills

A | Drafting

1 Answers may vary. Suggested answer:
1 c   2 e   3 d   4 g   5 h   6 a   7 b   8 f
In a topic area you know well the steps might more logically be:
1 c   2 e   3 h   4 a   5 d   6 g   7 b   8 f

2 Answers will vary
3 Answers will vary
4 Answers will vary
5 Answers will vary

B | Revising

1 Answers will vary
2 Introduction: 7, 8, 11, 14
   Paragraphs: 6, 13, 15, 16
   Conclusion: 1, 4, 12
   Language: 2, 10
   Sources: 3, 5, 9
3 Does my essay answer the question?
4 Answers will vary

Research task

Answers will vary in this section.

ACKNOWLEDGEMENTS

*The authors and publisher are grateful to those who have given permission to reproduce
the following extracts and adaptations of copyright material:* pp.5–6 From 'The
transcultural manager' by Karl Moore, p.72 of *World Business*, October 2006.
Reproduced by permission of Haymarket Worldwide; p.10 and pp.38–39 From
Introduction to Human Resource Management by Pinnington & Edwards (2000)
1583 words from pp.95–98, 195–197. By permission of Oxford University
Press; pp.15–16 From *Global Strategic Management* by Mellahi, Frynas, & Finley
(2011) 1034 words from pp.319–321. By permission of Oxford University Press;
pp.21–22 From *Corporate Governance* by Mallin (2010) 1068 words from pp.1–3.
By permission of Oxford University Press; pp.27–28 and pp.53–54 From *Oxford
Handbook of Personnel Psychology* edited by Cartwright & Cooper (2008) 2063 words
from pp.1–3, 93–120. By permission of Oxford University Press; pp.33–34 From
Oxford Handbook of International Business 2nd Edition edited by Rugman (2010) 863
words from pp.313–314. By permission of Oxford University Press; pp.43–44
From *Business Environment in a Global Context* by Harrison (2010) 1149 words
from pp.123–125. By permission of Oxford University Press; pp.48–49 From
Global Marketing Management 2nd Edition Lee & Carter (2009) 974 words from
pp.231–234. By permission of Oxford University Press; pp.59–60 From *How to
Change the World 2nd Edition* by Bornstein (2007) 791 words from pp.156–158. By
permission of Oxford University Press; pp.64–65 From *Marketing 2nd Edition* by
Baine, Fill & Page (2010) 837 words from pp.760, 762–763. By permission of
Oxford University Press; p.20 Entries from the *Oxford Business English Dictionary
for learners of English* © Oxford University Press; p.63 Entries from the *Oxford
Advanced Learner's Dictionary, 8th edition* © Oxford University Press.

Cover photograph by: Gareth Boden Photography

Illustrations by: Stefan Chabluk pp.15, 48. Rob Briggs p.38

The publishers would like to thank the following for permission to use their photographs:
Alamy Images pp.27 (Businesspeople/Chris Ryan), 39 (Business people writing
on a white board/Yuri Arcurs); Corbis pp.5 (Young businessman/Ocean),
10 (Business man at foot of steps/Dave & Les Jacobs), 16 (Business Meeting/
Ocean); Getty Images pp.22 (Former Enron Vice President/New York Daily News
Archive), 33 (Business people/Chris Ryan), 43 (Johannesburg Stock Exchange
trading floor/John Lamb), 53 (Business people in office/Jon Feingersh), 54 (Podium
speaker/Hill Street Studios), 59 (Queen Sofia of Spain/Farjana K. Godhuly),
60 (World Information Society Award/Fabrice Coffrini); Rex Features p.21 (IG
Markets/Rex Features); The Advertising Archives pp.64 (Mini Cooper posters/
The Advertising Archives), 65 (Mini Cooper poster/The Advertising Archives).